E.M. Forster's
A Passage to India

E.M. Forster's
A Passage to India

Edited by
Reena Mitra

ATLANTIC
PUBLISHERS & DISTRIBUTORS (P) LTD

Published by

ATLANTIC

PUBLISHERS & DISTRIBUTORS (P) LTD

7/22, Ansari Road, Darya Ganj, New Delhi-110002
Phones : +91-11-40775252, 23273880, 23275880, 23280451
Fax : +91-11-23285873
Web : www.atlanticbooks.com
E-mail : orders@atlanticbooks.com
Branch Office
5, Nallathambi Street, Wallajah Road, Chennai-600002
Phones : +91-44-64611085
E-mail : chennai@atlanticbooks.com

Printed in India at Nice Printing Press, A-33/3A, Site-IV,
Industrial Area, Sahibabad, Ghaziabad, U.P.

Preface

No introduction to E.M. Forster's *A Passage to India* can substitute for a close and thorough reading of the text for the reverberations and implications emanating from the work are multiple and, one might even say, intractable. For any kind of gratifying comprehension of the novel and the maze of interpretations of the work offered by the various critics one needs a meticulous and focused approach to it. Spirited and enthusiastic readers have been consistently drawn to the novel that defies reason and yet promises a world of meaning.

Forster began *A Passage to India*, his last completed novel, after his initial visit to India in 1912-13 but the work had to be abandoned in 1914 as he found it difficult to decide upon the essential nature of the consequential events and the subsequent ordeals that were to be experienced in the Marabar Caves. It was in 1921-22 that Forster visited India for a second time and worked for a few months as secretary to the Maharajah of Dewas State Senior. It was his experiences during his tenure here that provided material for the completion of the novel in 1924; it was a revived upsurge of consciousness regarding the complexities of Indian life at a time of soaring social fermentation that revitalized his creative imagination, enabling him to conclude the work.

A Passage to India was first published by Edward Arnold towards the close of 1924. The most authoritative and definitive edition of the novel, however, is Volume Six of the Collected Abinger edition of E.M. Forster's works published by Edward Arnold and edited by Oliver Stallybrass in 1979. This edition provides all the available manuscript variations, appendices and full notes—some by Forster himself—and an exhaustive introduction by Stallybrass.

A Passage to India centring around the British Raj, is set in Chandrapore, a town on the Ganges in north-eastern India. The thrust is on the Marabar Caves that impart a bewildering and inscrutable experience to the members of the ill-fated expedition, especially the

British Mrs. Moore and Adela Quested. Readers have incessantly been drawn to the enigma of the intimidating Caves and their resounding 'bou-oum' which defies reason yet continues to vex and activate the imagination. The various analyses that have followed the probing of the unsolved mystery at the heart of the novel have emanated from and have been fostered by the oblique and reflexive communication qualifying the text of the novel.

The voice with which Forster has reached out to his readers over decades is an unambiguous one that underscores the centrality in life of the individual and his personal relations and of the significance of forbearance, understanding and sympathy in an increasingly dismal existence. Forster has undauntedly exposed the oppression born of authority and demonstrated the consequences of "the undeveloped heart" which he believes is specifically characteristic of the British.

Forster, imbued with a sense of liberation, a marked contrast to English oppressive traditionalism, was always for men acting spontaneously and letting the artificial barriers separating them collapse magically, paving the way for a state of blissful harmony. And yet, he eludes categories and types. As John Maynard Keynes puts it in his work, *Two Memoirs*, he is "the elusive colt of a dark horse"; this phrase being generally indicative of Forster's essential inclination towards privacy and aversion to grading.

Forster finds in the harmony of art and order a culmination of the best man has attained and the highest he may aspire to in the face of the heightening disintegration in his cosmos. Art and order are the primary concerns pertinent to an understanding of Forster's world and are significant means of giving shape to an otherwise amorphous bulk of experiences and encounters.

I am thankful to all the contributors who have worked hard to present their papers. I also extend my thanks to Atlantic Publishers and Distributors (P) Ltd. for publishing this book. It will prove highly useful to the students and teachers of English literature and the researchers on E.M. Forster, particularly *A Passage to India*.

Reena Mitra

Contents

Preface   v

1. E.M. Forster: *A Passage to India*   1
   — *Reena Mitra*

2. Quest for Human Harmony in Forster's *A Passage to India*   23
   — *Sunita Sinha*

3. *A Passage to India* as Modernist Narrative : A Study   33
   — *Sreemati Mukherjee*

4. Gender, Race and Sexuality: Shifting Otherness
   in E.M. Forster's *A Passage to India*   48
   — *Shikha Misra*

5. The Soul's Voyage in Forster's *A Passage to India*   56
   — *Alka Saxena*

6. Cultural Misunderstandings in *A Passage to India*   64
   — *Neeta Shukla*

7. Thesis, Anti-thesis and Synthesis in Forster's
   A Passage to India   70
   — *Nivedita Tandon*

8. E.M. Forster's *A Passage to India* in Jhumpa Lahiri's
   Short Story, "Interpreter of Maladies"   77
   — *Susanna Ghazvinizadeh*

9. E.M. Forster's *A Passage to India:*
   A Study in Ecological Concerns
   — *Ram Narayan Panda*   86

10. Forster's Views on Art and the Novel   94
    —*Vinita Jha*

Contributors   108

1

E.M. Forster: *A Passage to India*
Reena Mitra

The growing critical interest in Forster's works since the fifties and the existing body of interpretative analyses on the various aspects of his novels, especially *A Passage to India*, is a comment on the richness and complexity of his literary achievements. Modern criticism has now, at last, given him his due; he has reached "classic status"[1] and has been fully entrenched as a major English author of the twentieth century. His eminence, however, it must be recognized, rests not on his artistic endeavour alone but on his philosophical pursuits and his quest for truth as well.

Forster believed that traditionally, "the novel tells a story... ", but he wished "that it was not so, that it could be something different—melody or perception of truth...".[2] He tried to make his own novels "something different".

The literary influences on Forster's aesthetic have been numerous. He himself has spoken of his indebtedness to several writers: "Samuel Butler influenced me a great deal.... He, Jane Austen and Marcel Proust are the three authors who have helped me most over my writing...."[3] Critics like Bradbury and Gransden have drawn attention to his Bloomsbury connection which inspired him with the ideals of the contemplation of beauty in art and the cultivation of personal relations. Others like Rose Macaulay, Trilling and Crews have emphasized his Victorian liberalism and humanism. Forster stands in a strange relation to the Liberal tradition for though he had long been committed to its ideas of progress, pragmatism, collectivism and humanitarianism, he could never really cultivate the liberal imagination which always looks for ideals and absolutes and refuses to take cognizance of the moral realism seen in the co-existence of opposites like good and evil. Another divergence from the Liberal tradition which sustained Forster's art was the ideal of self-cultivation as opposed to that of the "greatest-happiness", which was espoused by most Liberals.

In spite of the labels like 'liberal' and 'individualist' attached to him, "It is a dangerous game to pin E.M. Forster down"[4] warns Arnold Kettle. In 1927, I.A. Richards referred to Forster's quality of "oddness" deriving from his "unusual outlook on life" and pronounced him to be "the most puzzling figure in contemporary English letters".[5] Virginia Woolf also found "something baffling and evasive in the very nature of his gifts" and for her he failed to cohere into a single vision the mysticism and fact presented in his novels.[6] Lionel Trilling, in his influential study of Forster[7] saw him as a moral realist, though an evasive one, and believed that Forster's comic manner is the vehicle for a complex moral design. We may, then, define Forster's genius in the very same words that he used when writing about André Gide in 1943: "He has remained an individualist in an age which imposes discipline.... He's subtle and elusive."[8]

A Passage to India, an outcome of the two visits of Forster to the country in 1912-13 and 1920 respectively, is unanimously regarded as the culmination of the author's literary achievement. The title of the novel has been taken from Walt Whitman's famous poem, 'Passage to India'. The presence of an indefinite article in the title of Forster's novel is significant as it suggests that out of the multiple passages to India, this is distinctively Forster's own—an individualistic and liberal "passage" to the country; in fact, it is, as Whitman writes in his poem, a "Passage to more than India!"

As Middleton Murry observes, "A truly great novel is a tale to the simple, a parable to the wise, and a direct revelation of reality to the man who has made it a part of his being."[9] *A Passage to India* seems to conform to this definition of a great novel for it certainly tells a story, it presents in parable a case for tolerance and liberalism, and, with considerable success, attempts "a direct revelation of reality" as pertaining to human life.

A Passage to India is a novel as intricate as life itself and has the "eminently complex"[10] flavour of a Forster novel. Critics still continue to debate its meaning. At one level of interpretation, however, the book is clearly about the Anglo-Indians and about the Indians in British India but to overemphasize the socio-political elements in the novel would be to provide too simplistic an approach to a novel full of complexities of meaning. And yet, the political insights are not to be overlooked for the impact of imperialism on the development of characters and relationships is vital.

Characteristically, in *A Passage to India*, the plot and story are not co-extensive as they are in all the other novels of Forster. The plot is simple, precise and well-defined. The story, more expansive, precedes and extends beyond the plot in time. It does, no doubt, emanate from the plot itself and sounds the plot's manifold reverberation but it is far greater in its inclusiveness. The plot is conclusive but the story remains unresolved, an impulse, a perception which sets one thinking. The progression of events in the plot is causal and logical—all riddles are solved and everything is neatly wound up. The import of the story remains a mystery, a muddle, for the story is suffused with the theme of Hinduism, which is the most evasive of religions.

Thus runs the plot: Adela Quested arrives in India with Mrs. Moore, whose son by a first marriage she is going to marry. Both the ladies express a keen desire to "know India". This annoys Mrs. Moore's son, Ronny, and draws contempt from the other Anglo-Indians of Chandrapore. Mrs. Moore and Adela, on the other hand, disapprove of Ronny's adoption of the attitude of the ruling race and despite the latter's fuss about matters of propriety, Mrs. Moore enters a mosque one evening and there makes acquaintance with Aziz, a young Moslem doctor. Aziz, who has just been slighted by two English ladies, is pacified and soothed by Mrs. Moore's kindness. A friendship between the two develops and Adela, too, in course of time, becomes favourably disposed towards Aziz. Aziz, himself, is delighted at the prospect of the relationship and to convey his warmth to the two ladies organizes an elaborate excursion to the Marabar Caves. Cyril Fielding, the Principal of the local college at Chandrapore, and Professor Godbole, a Hindu teacher, are also to join them but they miss the train and Aziz goes ahead with the others. In one of the caves that she enters, Mrs. Moore has a disquieting psychic experience after which she decides to discontinue the exploration and let Adela and Aziz proceed without her. Adela, disturbed about the realization that she does not love the man she is to marry, ventures to speak of love to Aziz and offends him by asking certain personal questions. Aziz, annoyed, enters one of the caves and Adela goes into another. In the darkness of the cave, the strap of Adela's field glasses is pulled and broken by someone and she frantically runs out of the cave imagining that Aziz has attempted to assault her sexually. The English residents of Chandrapore are wild with rage when Adela makes the accusation and have no misgivings about Aziz's guilt. Only Fielding and Mrs. Moore are sure that Adela has been a victim of hallucination and that the incident could never have happened. Fielding, who declares his faith in Aziz, is boycotted, and Mrs. Moore, who only hints at Aziz's innocence, is promptly sent back to England by her son but owing to the unbearable heat, she dies on the way back home. At the trial, Adela's illusion is suddenly dispelled and she revokes her charge against Aziz. Aziz is acquitted, Fielding excused and given a better designation. The Indians rejoice at their victory while the English are furious with rage.

The plot, then, is devised with rare ingenuity for it provides tremendous opportunities for a study of both, the English and the native society. It exposes the initially latent, but later flagrant, antagonisms between the rulers and the ruled. The Anglo-Indian people come fully alive in all their hauteur and insensitivity and the Indians in all their humility. As Trilling points out, "by reason of the undeveloped heart",[11] the English are shown to have irretrievably lost their chances of retaining their hold over India.

In spite of all the expertise shown by Forster in the handling of the plot one often feels that the chain of events depicted in the novel is too frail and inadequate to carry the weight of the larger philosophical import. Hence the incongruity between the novel's inconsequential action and its metaphysical implications. The discerning reader, however, recognizes the fact that the sense of incongruity in the novel is only a reflection of the actual incongruous situation in life, that is, the pervasive irreconciliability between aspiration and reality. As E.K. Brown, the well-known American critic puts it, the principal idea of *A Passage to India* is "the chasm between the world of actions and the world of being".[12]

The novel, then, is not merely a piece of anti-colonial fiction but a modern classic as well, as relevant to the present times as it was to the period between the two World Wars. It pertains to the quest for enduring values in a disordered and divided world. The India that Forster depicts, with its multiplicity of conflicting races, creeds and religions, is a microcosm of the splintered world of the present century. The novel is an exploration of the possibilities of harmony and order in this world. Significantly enough, Forster never does affirm any such conceivable possibilities.

The theme of insurmountable barriers between races, sexes and cultures is what dominates every relationship in the novel but it is the chasm between the English and the Indians that is most dramatically presented. Aziz and Godbole, Adela and Ronny, Adela and Fielding, Mrs. Moore and Adela, Fielding and Stella, are all separated from each other in some way or the other. The most central relationship, however, is that between Fielding and Aziz, both of whom, in spite of the best of intentions and efforts, fail to achieve a lasting union, to communicate and to connect.

The theme of the novel, at the literal level, is stated at the very outset, that is, at the beginning of the second chapter, the brief opening chapter merely setting the scene and providing the backcloth to the action which ensues. The two Moslems with whom Aziz is dining, we are told "were discussing as to whether or no it is possible to be friends with an Englishman".[13] This is exactly what the novel is about. Arnold Kettle in his critical analysis of *A Passage to India* writes, "it is typical of Forster to make no bones about stating his theme. The actual words of the statement are important. They are down to earth and they are precise."[14] Forster, Kettle goes on to say, is too sensible to attempt to decontextualize relationships and to present characters as removed from time and place, and hence, the particular context of life in British India.

Forsters faith in personal relations is very clear from his credo as spelt out in 'What I Believe': "I hate the idea of causes and if I had to choose between betraying my country and betraying my friend, I hope I should have the guts to betray my country."[15] His ardent belief in the values of the inner life are best expressed in the words of Helen in *Howard's End*:

> ...I knew it (union with Paul) was impossible, because
> personal relations are the important thing for ever and
> ever and not this outer life of telegrams and anger.[16]

The one hope for unity, then, according to Forster, is a trust in the power of friendly personal relations among individuals; but, even this proves inadequate as we see in the relationship between Aziz and Fielding. The more sincere the advances of personal goodwill, the more they are misinterpreted on either side. The responsibility for the failure of communication rests not on the individuals but upon human nature in general and upon "the whole conflict of civilizations"[17] as Crews observes. And Forster in *A Passage to India*, instead of recommending a way of behaviour, simply tries to show us an image of our miserable plight as human beings, engaged in a losing battle against the meaninglessness of life.

The tripartite structure of *A Passage to India* has invited various interpretative explanations from different critics and it is for the reader to make his choice regarding the one to subscribe to. The novelist's own clue to the interpretation, however, cannot be ignored. Forster, in the "Author's Notes" to the Everyman edition of the novel, writes, "The three sections— Mosque, Caves, Temple—represent the three seasons of the

Indian year—winter, summer and the rains."[18] This seasonal setting of the three sections suggests the mood and the frame of mind of the various characters as also the spirit of the situations in the novel.

R.A. Brower,[19] finding corroboration in Forster's own introductory note to the novel, has dealt with the symbolic significance of the work at length and concentrated on "a group of symbolic metaphors" which compose "the central design" of *A Passage to India*. 'Mosque', the first section, he believes, is associated with arch; 'Caves', the second section, with echo, and 'Temple', the third, with sky.

Gertrude White, building up her arguments on the theme of "fission and fusion"[20] in the novel, interprets the three parts of *A Passage to India* as an aesthetic rendition of the Hegelian triad—"Thesis—Antithesis—Synthesis", or, the statement of the problem and two opposite resolutions. Glen O. Allen,[21] rejecting Gertrude White's Hegelian interpretation, identifies the tripartite structural design of the novel with three notions of Indian philosophy, viz., the ways of Dhyan (Knowledge), Karma (Work) and Bhakti (Love).

John Colmer[22] in his critique of the novel refers to the dialectical structure of the novel consisting of positive affirmation (Mosque), negative retraction (Caves) and muted reaffirmation (Temple). Frederick C. Crews suggests that various religious paths to the ultimate truth of life are being "problematically offered" in the novel only to suggest through the inconclusive ending that all paths lead to a frustrating maze.[23]

Peter Burra has a completely different interpretation of the three-fold structure of *A Passage to India*. According to him, the novel with its three parts, is planned like a symphony in three movements "that are given their shape and their interconnections by related and contrasted localities". The "Marabar Caves" are the keynote in the symphony to which the melody keeps returning. Before the cave incident the repeated reference to the Caves leads us forward to the disaster. After the happening, every mention of the caves takes us back to the centre, "to the mystery that is never solved". 'Mosque', 'Caves' and 'Temple' represent man's spiritual explorations in the world.[24]

Shahane's elucidation[25] of the three divisions of the novel is based on the idea of personal relationships. 'Mosque', the first section, poses the question of the possibilities of personal communion and friendship; in 'Caves', the second section, the answer to the question posed in the first is given in terms of negativity and chaos. 'Temple', the third section, gives us the final solution to the problem stated. The message that the novel seems to convey is that love alone devoid of mysticism is incapable of resolving the moral and spiritual problems of humanity.

The multifarious explications of this three-fold edifice of *A Passage to India* that have come forth bear testimony to the fact that the novel has been a successful thought-provoking literary venture. The titles of the three parts of the novel—"Mosque", "Caves", "Temple"—warn us of a meaning which goes far beyond the plot, characters and setting. They indicate the religious preoccupations of the work. In the first section, the Moslem Aziz meets Mrs. Moore in a mosque; in the section of the Marabar caves the central situation of the novel is developed; and, in the final section, there is a symbolic exposition of the Hindu view of the universe. This last section is also in the nature of an epilogue presenting the parting of Aziz and Fielding.

Each of the three parts of the novel has a significant prefatory chapter and each of these chapters has an abundance of symbolic clues, which, if rightly construed, help in a proper understanding of the implications of the work. Clearly, these prefatory chapters are interrelated and interweave the main strands of the novel. The introductory chapter of "Mosque" begins and ends with a reference to the Marabar Caves. The opening words are "Except for the Marabar Caves...", and the chapter closes with "These fists and fingers are the Marabar Hills, containing the extra-ordinary caves." There is, in it, a casual reference to the temples in Chandrapore, too, but the casualness is only a facade for the designed introduction to a word that carries so much weight. The mosque is mentioned only in the title for this part.

The first chapter of the section called "Caves" does not refer to the mosque or the Moslem religion at all but contains implicit remarks regarding the temple and the Hindu faith. And yet, in contrast, the chapter deals mainly with an account of a primitive India far older than the Moslem or Hindu India—the ancient India that was prior to and above any religion and marked by an "unspeakable"[26] quality.

In the initial chapter of the third part of the tripartition called "Temple" the start is made, as in "Mosque", with a mention of the caves. The Moslem element is brought in by the importance in the chapter of the action of the chief Moslem character in the novel, Aziz. This intermingling of elements in these prefatory chapter, it must be remembered, has been accomplished with the greatest of subtlety and is no mere haphazard balancing of form, "Vitality", as L.K. Brown discriminatingly observes, "is not sacrificed to pattern".[27]

Thus, the prefatory chapters can best be looked upon as a group and their interdependence suggests a consolidated approach to the three sections, or "blocks"[28] as Brown calls them. Any attempt at making a chapter-wise analysis of the novel is promptly thwarted for there is a progressive increase in the complexity of the work and the only approach that is rewarded with response and enlightenment is the approach to the aesthetic endeavour, as a whole. In the first part, the Moslem element dominates—the cages and the temple are only referred to in passing though the reference as we see later, is of potential value. In the third part, however, the Hindu element dominates but the persistence of the Moslem and of the primitive and evasive element of the caves cannot be ignored.

The first section, "Mosque", sets the scene—Chandrapore, a British station—for the action in the novel and introduces the main characters. The opening chapter, as already explained, is purely descriptive, and anticipatory in nature but meaningfully enough, it establishes a number of striking contrasts: between the cool, objective mind of the author and the hot brewing "muddle" that India is; between the "low but indestructible form of life"[29] of the natives and the organized but barren life of the English; between the disharmony on the earth and the possibility of harmony suggested by the overarching sky"[30] that "settles everything".[31]

Aziz, after an unpleasant confrontation with his superior, Major Callendar, the Civil Surgeon, enters the mosque to regain his composure. Mrs. Moore, finding the atmosphere in the club rather stifling approaches the mosque alone. Aziz's encounter with Mrs. Moore in the subdued light of the lamp in the mosque is central to the book. She respects him, sympathizes for the wrongs done to him and tells him of her instinctive liking for and aversion to certain people. Aziz happily responds with "Then you are an Oriental",[32] and his words prove prophetic. Already, she is estranged from the Anglo-Indians of Chandrapore and even from Adela, who herself wants to see "the real India".[33] Her inclinations are more towards Aziz, whose indiscretions regarding Major Callendar she asks her son to keep to himself as she does not wish to betray Aziz's confidence in her. She has come out of the mosque believing in personal relations, which the Anglo-Indian world does not value. Later in the section, when going to hang her cloak, she notices a wasp on the peg and her reaction to the wasp—the Indian wasp—as "pretty dear"[34] is indication of her expansive heart that now finds the Christian tendency to exclude too narrow as compared to the Hindu inclusiveness. The wasp, as a part of India, a part of the universe, recurs in the mind of Godbole much later in the novel in the third section.

To Ronny's insistence that the English are not in India to be pleasant, Mrs. Moore's personal and typically Oriental argument is:

> The English *are* out here to be pleasant...because India
> is part of the earth. And God has put us on the earth to
> be pleasant to each other. God...is...love.[35]

These very words, "God is love", are chanted again in the third part of the novel, at the Hindu religious festival presided over by Godbole, who later reiterates Mrs. Moore's views by saying that God is present in the good. Mrs. Moore's thoughts since her arrival in India have been increasingly centred around God, God gradually becoming to her more elusive and less definable: "Outside the arch, there seemed always an arch, beyond the remotest echo of silence."[36] The word 'echo' here anticipates the echo in the caves which are central to the second part of the novel. In fact, the whole novel is, as Trilling puts it, a "reticulation of echoes".[37]

Aziz, to please Mrs. Moore and Miss Quested, invites them along with Fielding and Godbole, to a picnic at the Marabar Caves. Before this, they assemble for a party at Fielding's house, where Godbole sings a religious song about the visitation of Krishna and concludes with "He refuses to come" which implies the vagueness and elusiveness of God. The negativity of life, as symbolized by the hollow rock, the Kawa Dol, is brought home to us through Godbole's projection of the nondescript quality of the caves—the caves that provide no positive affirmation of life.

The second part of the book gives the visit to the caves, and suggestively enough, Fielding and Godbole miss the train because the latter takes too long praying. Before the actual experience in the caves Forster succeeds in conveying a sense of the impending disaster. The episode of the caves is the very core of the novel, the "area in which concentration can take place".[38]

What is important about the caves is the effect they have on people in "certain conditions of receptivity".[39] The heat is considerable and the two ladies start on the excursion in a mood of apathy. The caves retort with a blurring of impressions and a total frustrating of reason and form. Mrs. Moore grows more withdrawn after her unpleasant claustrophobic experience in one of the caves and personal relations, which were once most important for her, now cease to matter. The "echo" in the cave brings upon Mrs. Moore's consciousness the realization that "Pathos, piety, courage—they exist, but are identical, and so is filth. Everything exists, nothing has value."[40] The echo for her is the indifference of God which answers everything with "boum" and a realization of this indifference which replaced her faith in "God is love" frightens her into resignation and causes a disintegration of her personality.

Adela is a young, rational woman with little experience of life and, thus, unable to come to terms with the 'echo', becomes a victim of hallucination. Her experience in the cave, though religious in implications, is more amenable to a psychological interpretation. Mrs. Moore's thoughts, when entering the Cave, are on religion and so, for her, the echo is a religious revelation. Adela's yearnings are sexual, not mystical. She is perturbed by the realization that she is not in love with her fiancé, Ronny, and hence, for her the echo is the emptiness of life without physical love. Her hallucination (if that is what it is) of being sexually assaulted by Aziz is just a virgin's fancy in the heat of the day, imagining a rape she secretly desired. Adela, however, lacks the imagination to be permanently undermined by her inexplicable experience.

In *A Passage to India*, the description of the minds of the two British women after their psychic experience in the cave is the most difficult task that Forster assigns himself. The depiction, however, is admirably managed. Adela's breakdown is an effective method of dramatizing her sudden confrontation with forces she had never recognized in life and her inability to cope with them. Her rational, commonsense approach is totally inapplicable to the echo which haunts her mind for so long.

What is significant about the caves is their symbolic value. They represent the individual mind and whatever happens in them—good or evil—is what is brought to them by the individual. They reflect the minds of all who enter them and their subconscious fears and desires. John Colmer suggests that the entry into the caves may be taken as representing a descent into the subconscious.[41] In other words, it is the extreme subjectivity of truth that is stressed.

At a broader level, the incidents in the caves represent India's imposition of its force of illusion and disillusion upon the British visitors making the incompatibility between the East and the West appear more real and vivid. At a still more expansive level of meaning, India represents the whole of creation and to understand India is to comprehend the rationale of the whole of creation. The problems of India are the problems of all human life and the caves are symbolically, "the focus of experience and the judgement on experience".[42]

The precise interpretation of the caves is the most intricate problem of any critical appreciation of *A Passage to India*. From Forster's own preface to the Everyman edition of the novel we learn that the Marabar is another name for the Barabar Caves situated near Gaya in North-

East India. Though *The Imperial Gazetteer of India*, 1908, contains references to the association of the Barabar Caves with Buddhism, Forster deliberately dissociates the Marabar Caves from any particular religion so as to emphasize their cosmic and universal nature as also their mysterious and symbolic character.

Critics have a variety of interpretations of the symbolic nature of the Caves. Gertrude White believes the Marabar to be "the very voice of that union which is the opposite of divine; the voice of evil and negation".[43] Virginia Woolf thinks that they "...may be the soul of India".[44] Austin Warren finds them "bare, dark, echoing eternity, infinity, the Absolute",[45] whereas Lionel Trilling likens them to "Wombs"[46] in view of the radical responses they give rise to in Mrs. Moore and Adela. E.K. Brown speaks of the characteristic quality of the echo of the Marabar cave—the quality of complete meaninglessness.[47]

According to John Sayre Martin, when Forster refers to all sounds emitted in the cave being answered with the same "boum", he is stretching physical plausibility too far but his purpose is to make a symbolic point— the point that all value is totally subjective and having no transcendent confirmation, is equally meaningless. The caves' echoes, themselves, make a ruinous impression only on Mrs. Moore and Adela. Professor Godbole, Fielding and Aziz either never hear the echo or are never really impressed by it, perhaps, because they are sure of their spiritual values and act in accordance with them. Mrs. Moore and Adela have both been undergoing a spiritual crisis since their arrival in India. Mrs. Moore begins to doubt the adequacy of the Christian faith in comprehending the muddle and mystery around her and Adela is unable to decide as to whether or not to marry Ronny, whom she does not really love. So, "Just as the echo is an objective correlative for Mrs. Moore's crisis of faith, so it is the same for Adela's crisis of conduct."[48]

Just as there is a variety of critical opinion on the symbolic nature of the caves, so, too, there is a lot of speculation regarding what really happened in the caves. Forster's own explanation of this in a letter to G.L. Dickinson in 1924 was:

> In the cave it is *either* a man, or the supernatural, *or* an illusion. And even if I know ! My writing mind therefore is a blur here—i.e. I will it to remain a blur, and to be uncertain, as I am of many facts in daily life. This isn't a philosophy of aesthetics. It's a particular trick I felt justified in trying because my theme was India. It sprang from my subject matter. I wouldn't have attempted it in other countries, which though

> they contain mysteries or muddles, manage to draw
> rings round them.[49]

Later, in 1934, in a review of a novel by William Plomer, Forster expressed that he had "tried to show that India is an unexplainable muddle by introducing an unexplained muddle—Miss Quested's experience in the cave".[50] When asked what had happened there, Forster's reply was, "I don't know".[51] Because of Forster's reluctance to explain Adela's experience, we are still, as Louise Dauner puts it, "literally and metaphorically, in the dark as to what really happened to Adela Quested in the cave; and yet this episode is the structural core of the novel".[52]

Thus, though "the caves are central both structurally and thematically" and "out of them emanates the novel's meaning...",[53] there is no consensus of opinion regarding what really took place in the caves. Most critics, however, agree that Adela had a hallucinatory experience that she perceived as rape—this was Fielding's suggestion in the novel itself. Yet, Adela herself never fully accepts this explanation and keeps implying that it may have been the guide.[54] Jo Ann Hoeppner Moran, however, does not believe in Forster's own ignorance regarding what happens in the caves. In fact, he points out that Forster does tell us what transpired in the caves although "in a typically subtle and elusive way, spacing out the clues to the solution through the text".[55]

The closing chapter of Part II of the novel describes Fielding's voyage back to England, away from the strange, the extraordinary, back to the Mediterranean norm. It appears as if the book is about to come to an end for what reconciliation could there be after such estrangement? None, perhaps, on the physical and active plane. But then, in the third part of the novel there is, as Gransden puts it, a "Kierkegaardian 'qualitative leap' "[56] on to another plane altogether—the religious and the spiritual. The brief finale in Part III is structurally essential to the novel for in it the threads are woven together into a pattern, which, though not conclusive, is aesthetically fascinating.

At the very beginning of "Temple", the final section of the novel, the theme of the last movement of the symphony is conveyed:

> Some hundreds of miles westward of the Marabar
> caves, and two years later in time, Professor Narayan
> Godbole stands in the presence of God. God is not
> born yet—that will occur at midnight—but He has
> also been born centuries ago, nor can He ever be born,

because He is the Lord of the Universe, who transcends human processes.[57]

In the gripping description of the Krishna festival which follows, there are strains of light-heartedness, even absurdity, which are part of the Hindu inclusiveness allowing "the inclusion of merriment".[58] The reader is amused when he is told that the local draughtsman's spelling of the English slogan contained "an unfortunate slip": 'God is love'.[59] In spite of all this entertainment the description remains a powerful one, the power being derived through the presence of Godbole, the Hindu believer.

At the festival only the Hindus are important; the Moslems and the English do not matter for to them the festival is a muddle, as the caves were. Yet, the uncertainties aroused by the caves can be sorted out only by the temple, not by the mosque or the church, both of which believe in a personal romantic creed. The Hindu devotees, in their moment of communion with God, assume "a beauty in which there was nothing personal, for it caused them all to resemble each other during the moment of its indwelling".[60] The divine annihilates all distinctions: Mrs. Moore's vision, the echo in the caves, was true: with the birth of Lord Krishna, sorrow is dispelled for all, Indians as well as "foreigners, birds, caves, railways, and the stars"[61]—all creation is one and shares in joy. Godbole, now at the culmination of his spiritual experience, has a vision of Mrs. Moore, who is a part of infinite love. Her form of Christianity is purer than the narrow one practised in Forster's Anglo-India. It is basically a religion of love blended with a mystical sense of the divine. It allows her to cross the barriers of race and creed and make friends with Aziz but it is yet inadequate to comprehend the "muddle" that India is.

Aziz thinks of Mrs. Moore as an Oriental, the ignorant Indian crowd takes her to be a demi-goddess. What is more important is Godbole's view of her, Godbole who experiences a strange sense of kinship with her. In an inspired state of devotion, he remembers "an old woman",[62] whom chance brought into his mind. In the same spiritual experience he sees her once again:

> He had, with increasing vividness again seen Mrs. Moore, and round her faintly clinging forms of trouble. He was a Brahman, she Christian, but it made no difference whether she was a trick of his memory or a telepathic appeal. It was his duty...to place himself in the position of the God and love her...and say...'Come, come, come, come'.[63]

Godbole and Mrs. Moore thus have in common their faith in love—selfless love—as an attribute of the Divine and their attraction towards the wasp which is indicative of the extension of their sympathies for all forms of life. This wasp had once drawn the attention of Mrs. Moore and later in the book, it appears as an image to Godbole. E.K. Brown, specifying the achievement of the recurrence of the wasp in the novel says that it "points to an identity in the objects to which the analogous characters are drawn".[64]

Islam the religion of Dr. Aziz, one of the major characters of *A Passage to India*, is treated more sympathetically. Having less of a nationalistic bias than Christianity, it inspires Aziz's sense of beauty and history, and moves him to write poetry on the glory of the Islamic past. This glory, however, has no relevance to the problems of the present times.

So, as compared to Islam and Christianity, Hinduism comes closest to resolving the confusions and problems of life in India. The temple-scene with all its chaos of music, revelry, noise and piety is representative of the muddle and mystery of India. It is by design that Forster places this scene immediately after the scene of Fielding's arrival in Venice, which, unlike India, stands for "the civilization that has escaped muddle, the spirit in a reasonable form, with flesh and blood subsisting".[65]

Hinduism, then, is at the core of the novel. Like India which has accommodated such a vast variety of cultures, creeds and races, Hinduism, too, has grown through on assimilation of the customs and beliefs of the native people as well as those of the invaders. This syncretistic trait of the religion is what Forster projects. In Mau, Aziz finds that a Moslem saint is worshipped by the Hindus and that the Moslems of the place had grown idolatrous under the influence of the Hindus. Mrs. Moore, the English lady, is transformed into "Esmiss Esmoor", a Hindu goddess.

Hinduism's all-inclusiveness conceives of a world in which the good and the evil, the preposterous and the exalted, the cruel and the kind co-exist. The Caves, we see, reconcile ideas of pacifism and violence. Forster, in his Paris Review interview has called the Caves a "good substitute for violence", but during the trial we are informed that the caves are Jain, Jainism being the most peace-loving sect within Hinduism. Hinduism also contains within itself the recognition of divisions among men and encourages men to eliminate such barriers and embrace all.

Lionel Trilling, in his study of Forster believes that Forster is inclined towards religion because "it expresses, though it does not solve, the human mystery".[66] This mystery which is identified with India, is embodied in Godbole. He is partly a comic figure, but a sort of wise fool, who represents the harmonious contradictions allowed for in Hinduism. As Benita Parry observes, "Godbole's energies are directed towards developing the life of the spirit"[67] and hence he is not fit for practical tasks like catching the train. He is the voice of the "bhakti" cult of the Hindus and the chief embodiment of love in its universal context.

The third section of the novel, "Temple", is highly significant in dramatizing the impact and limitations of universal love and recent criticism has pointed out its importance in the novel's structure and totality of meaning. Forster, himself, when asked at an interview about the exact function of the long description of the Hindu festival in *A Passage to India*, replied:

> It was architecturally necessary. I needed a lump, or a Hindu temple if you like—a mountain standing up. It is well-placed; and it gathers up some strings. But there ought to be more after it....[68]

Forster's opinion of Hinduism, as seen in the novel and as specifically pointed out by Crews, is clearly this: although Hinduism offers the most fascinating fable for the 'meaninglessness' in the world, and our isolation from meaning, it is as powerless as Islam or Christianity when confronted with the nihilistic message of the Marabar Caves. The indecisiveness and ambiguity of Forster's total vision is clear and his attitude to all religions remains one of agnosticism and sceptical detachment.

The failure of each of the main characters in his efforts to achieve harmony arises from an inability to love in a selfless manner as also from the insurmountable religious, social and cultural barriers. The last paragraph of the novel, recapitulating the main images of the book, gives in symbolic terms the ultimate failure of Aziz and Fielding to achieve a lasting harmony 'here' and 'now'.

Most of Forster's English characters are depicted as lacking in imagination and having an undeveloped heart which fails to reach out. Mrs. Moore and Fielding are the only two characters from whom we cannot withhold our sympathies. The depiction of English officials by Forster has, of course, been disputed in England but the fact remains that the reader cannot but look upon them with a certain degree of antipathy. The Indians, most of them, are conceived in sympathy and affection but are shown as lacking in dignity. Once, at his vindication feast, Aziz is represented as "full of civilization...complete, dignified, rather hard"[69] and for the first time Fielding is conscious of this exaltation, but this only shows Aziz's usual lack of dignity. Aziz is sketched as lively, impulsive, garrulous and sensitive to beauty. The human warmth in him makes it difficult for one to dislike the young Muslim doctor, and Mrs. Moore and Fielding, both look upon him with great affection.

Though lacking the qualities of a conventional heroine, Adela is shown to possess intellectual honesty and sincerity which make her an interesting and sympathetic character. Ronny is shown to us more through the comments of other people which enable the novelist to expose his deficiencies while still retaining sympathy for him as Adela's suitor. A definite deterioration in character has taken place since Ronny came to India but we never really come to hate him.

Fielding is described as a "hard-bitten, good-tempered intelligent fellow on the verge of middle-age, with a belief in education".[70] He speaks with a highly individual voice and remarks about the necessity of seeing Indians if one is to see the real India. He tells Adela, "I really do get on with Indians, and they do trust me."[71] His English reserve has already been broken down by Aziz's impulsiveness and he has come to feel genuinely for Indians. He has the breadth of experience that the English officials lack and like Forster himself he is antipathetic towards English women in India. As Colmer observes, "He has all the virtues of the liberal humanist: he believes in the supreme value of ideas, is free from race-feeling, remains detached, observant, skeptical, tolerant amid an intolerant passionate environment."[72] A rationalist, he cannot accept the irrational; he is unable to respond to the echo in the caves. In Fielding, Forster's views his own liberal humanistic creed objectively and recognizes its limitations.

As for Mrs. Moore, it is she who carries the theme of Hinduism in the novel in the sense that the theme is first introduced by her observation of the wasp. Later in the novel, though, the theme is passed on to Godbole. Mrs. Moore's discovery of the inadequacy of Christianity in dealing with the problems of life, bring her closer to the Indian ways of feeling. She is, as Aziz says, "an Oriental"[73] in her intuitive and impulsive response to things. She dominates the action in the novel and as "Esmiss Esmoor" becomes a Hindu goddess to the crown. Although she abandons her moral duty by going back to England when her evidence would have been crucial, she does, even in her absence, influence Adela to withdraw her charge against Aziz. She re-appears in the novel in the person of her son, Ralph Moore and the bond between Aziz and her is re-established when Aziz and Ralph become friends.

Godbole is at once impressive and ludicrous and we see him in his element at the Hindu festival at Mau. He is no humanist and loves God, not people. Towards people he is completely detached and totally inaccessible. God loves "all men, the whole universe"[74] but his is a completely impersonal love, the love of a saint or a mystic for the Divine. Godbole stands as Forster's standard of truth, elusive and impenetrable.

Comedy is an important aspect of Forster's art for it provides the necessary balance to his symbolism and keeps him from going too far into allegory. The author's private search for meaning is continually refreshed by his comic spirit which brings him back to the objective world. There is, of course, less of comedy in *A Passage to India* than there is in Forster's other novels, but even here we do have comic relief in Godbole's ridiculous mannerisms and in Aziz's excessive keenness to entertain his British guests well at the Marabar excursion.

An important characteristic of *A Passage to India* that draws attention is the dominance of the natural and the non-human world. All Forster's descriptions suggest that human life is dominated by the natural forces, by the earth and the sky. *A Passage to India* opens and ends with a sense of the omnipotence of the sky, which makes promise of a transcendent harmony but never does allow the removal of barriers between man and man. Thus, apart from the mental landscape that India offers to Forster as a background for the development of his themes in this novel, she also provides a sprawling, dominant, physical landscape that dwarfs the protagonist and challenges the established values of the West.

The sceptical note regarding the Aziz-Fielding relationship at the end of the novel is not, however, evidence of a defeatist attitude. It shows Forster as a moral realist visualizing what life ought to be and yet, conscious of what life really is. Love should prevail in human life but barriers are difficult to cross and man is doomed to remain isolated.

A Passage to India arouses infinite speculations. Is Forster offering the mysticism of Hinduism as a possible corrective to the drawbacks of individualism not just in India but in the world situation? Can this mystic religion be a salvation for a world destined to fragmentation by its own indiscretions? The message of the caves and the insights of the temple seem to be offered as a substitute to the assertiveness and complacence of the West.

It is the perfect balance of symbolic suggestion, comic-effect, psychological insight and social and moral realism that makes *A Passage to India* a satisfying novel. Forster's curious technique of juxtaposing, scenes of symbolic significance with those of comic-effect is perhaps to demonstrate that even comedy can take on a sober philosophical import. Aziz's embarking upon an expedition to the Marabar appears comic, and yet, it has grave consequences. Scenes of the religious ceremony at

Mau seem farcical and yet, they have a deep symbolic significance. Thus, Forster's manner, however comic, is the agent of a moral intention.

In the novel, Forster assumes the role of an omniscient narrator and shapes his prose for comment and explanation. Yet, consistency in point of view is not strictly adhered to. In the cave episode, for instance, Forster conveniently changes his stance from that of an omniscient storyteller to that of a detached observer. He often resorts to exaggeration and improbability for effect for he knows that verisimilitude does not always provide pleasure or truth. There is, sometimes, exaggeration in characterization as well as in the depiction of a scene. The portrayal of the English officials often appears to be exaggerated. The religious scene at the temple, too, may seem to be overdone.

On the whole, tone in the novel is deftly managed and direct authorial comments establish Forster's understanding of human existence, inspiring in the reader, confidence in his ironic but compassionate vision of life. Occasionally, however, his dual vision of the adequacy of Hinduism in dealing with the problems of life is disconcerting.

NOTES

1. Malcolm Bradbury, ed., "Introduction" *Forster: A Collection of Critical Essays* (New Delhi: Prentice Hall of India Pvt. Ltd., 1979), 14.

2. E.M. Forster, *Aspects of the Novel* (Harmondsworth: Penguin, 1962), 34.

3. John Sayre Martin, "Introduction", *E.M. Forster: The Endless Journey* (New Delhi: Vikas Publishing House, 1976), 11, cited from *Two Cheers for Democracy*.

4. Arnold Kettle, *An Introduction to the English Novel-II* (New Delhi: B.I. Publications, rpt. 1978), 137.

5. John Sayre Martin, *E.M. Forster : The Endless Journey*, 1.

6. Virginia Woolf, 'The Novels of E.M. Forster' in *Collected Essays*, Vol. I (London, 1966), 342-51.

7. Lionel Trilling, *E.M. Forster—A Study* (London: The Hogarth Press, 1944), 12.

8. E.M. Forster, *Two Cheers for Democracy* (London: Edward Arnold, 1951), 234.

9. Middleton Murry, "The Breakup of the Novel", 1924; cited in *Forster: A Collection of Critical Essays*, ed., Malcolm Bradbury, 90.

10. David Cecil, *Poets and Storytellers: A Book of Critical Essays* (London: Macmillan, 1949), 182.

11. Lionel Trilling, *E.M. Forster: A Study*.

12. E.K. Brown, "E.M. Forster and the Contemplative Novel", *University of Toronto Quarterly* III, April, 1934, 349-61.

13. E.M. Forster, *A Passage to India* (Harmondsworth: Penguin, rpt. 1969), 12.

14. Arnold Kettle, *An Introduction to the English Novel*, Vol. II, 137.

15. E.M. Forster, "What I Believe", 1939 (reprinted), *Two Cheers for Democracy*, 78.

16. E.M. Forster, *Howard's End* (London: Arnold, 1910), 184.

17. Frederick C. Crews, *The Perils of Humanism—A Study of E.M. Forster* (Princeton: Princeton University Press, 1961).

18. E.M. Forster, *A Passage to India* (London: Everyman, 1942), IX.

19. R.A. Brower, *The Fields of Light: An Experiment in Critical Reading* (New York, 1951), 182.

20. Gertrude M. White, "A Passage to India: Analysis and Revaluation", *PMLA*, LXVIII, September 1953, 64.

21. Glen O. Allen, "Structure, Symbol, and Theme in E.M. Forster's 'A Passage to India' ", *PMLA*, LXX, December 1955, 938.

22. John Colmer, *A Passage to India* (London: Edward Arnold, 1967).

23. Frederick C. Crews, *The Perils of Humanism—A Study of E.M. Forster*.

24. Peter Burra, "The Novels of E.M. Forster", *The Nineteenth Century and After*, CXVI (November, 1934), 581-94.

25. V.A. Shahane, *E.M. Forster: A Reassessment* (New Delhi: Kitab Mahal, 1962), 117.

26. E.M. Forster, *A Passage to India*, 123.

27. E.K. Brown, "Rhythm in E.M. Forster's 'A Passage to India'", *Forster: A Collection of Critical Essays*, ed. Malcolm Bradbury (New Delhi: Prentice Hall of India, 1979), 153.

28. *Ibid.*

29. E.M. Forster, *A Passage to India*, 9.

30. *Ibid.*, 10.

31. *Ibid.*

32. *Ibid.*, 24.

33. *Ibid.*, 25.

34. *Ibid.*, 35.
35. *Ibid.*, 51.
36. *Ibid.*, 51-52.
37. Lionel Trilling, *E.M. Forster—A Study.*
38. P.N. Furbank and F.J.H. Haskell, *Writers at Work*, The Paris Review Interviews, ed. Malcolm Cowley (New York: Viking Press, 1958), 26.
39. K.W. Gransden, *E.M. Forster* (New York: Oliver and Boyd, 1962), 92.
40. E.M. Forster, *A Passage to India*, 147.
41. John Colmer, *A Passage to India.*
42. K.W. Gransden, *E.M. Forster*, 93.
43. Gertrude White, "A Passage to India: Analysis and Revaluation", *PMLA*, LXVIII.
44. Virginia Woolf, *The Death of the Moth and Other Essays* (London: The Hogarth Press, 1942), 168.
45. Austin Warren, "E.M. Forster", *The American Review*, 1937.
46. Lionel Trilling, *E.M. Forster—A Study.*
47. E.K. Brown "Rhythm in E.M. Forster's 'A Passage to India'", *Forster: A Collection of Critical Essays*, ed. Bradbury, 149.
48. John Sayre Martin, *E.M. Forster: The Endless Journey*, 151.
49. P.N. Furbank, E.M. *Forster: A Life*, Vol. 2 (London: Seeker and Warburg, 1977), 125.
50. *Ibid.*
51. *Ibid.*
52. Louise Danner, "What Happened in the Cave? Reflections on 'A Passage to India' ", *Perspectives on E.M. Forster's 'A Passage to India*, ed. V.A. Shahane (New York: Barnes, 1968), 52-64.
53. Wilfrid Stone, *The Cave and the Mountain: A Study of E.M. Forster* (Stanford: Stanford University Press, 1966), 16.
54. E.M. Forster, *A Passage to India*, 235.
55. Jo Ann Hoeppner Moran, "E.M. Forster's 'A Passage to India': What Really Happened in the Caves", *Modern Fiction Studies*, Vol. 34, No. 4, Winter 1988, 598.
56. K.W. Gransden, *E.M. Forster*, 100.
57. E.M. Forster, *A Passage to India*, 279.
58. *Ibid.*, 284.
59. *Ibid.*, 281.

60. *Ibid.*, 280.

61. *Ibid.*, 283.

62. *Ibid.*, 281.

63. *Ibid.*, 285-86.

64. E.K. Brown, "Rhythm in E.M. Forster's 'A Passage to India'", *Forster: A Collection of Critical Essays*, ed. Malcolm Bradbury, 148.

65. E.M. Forster, *A Passage to India*, 275.

66. Lionel Trilling, *E.M. Forster—A Study.*

67. Benita Parry, "Passage to More than India", *Forster: A Collection of Critical Essays*, ed. Bradbury, 167.

68. P.N. Furbank and F.J.H. Haskell, *Writers at Work*, 27.

69. Frederick C. Crews, *The Perils of Humanism—A Study of E.M. Forster.*

70. E.M. Forster, *A Passage to India*, 244.

71. *Ibid.*, 61.

72. *Ibid.*, 257.

73. John Colmer, *E.M. Forster: A Passage to India.*

74. E.M. Forster, *A Passage to India*, 281.

BIBLIOGRAPHY

Primary Sources

Forster, E.M. *Howard's End.* London: Arnold, 1910.

—— *Two Cheers for Democracy.* London: Arnold, 1951.

—— *Aspects of the Novel.* Harmondsworth: Penguin, 1962.

—— *A Passage to India.* Harmondsworth: Penguin, rpt. 1969.

Secondary Sources

Allen, Glen O. 'Structure, Symbol and Theme in E.M. Forster's "A Passage to India"', *PMLA*, LXX, December 1955.

Bradbury, Malcolm. *Forster: A Collection of Critical Essays.* New Delhi: Prentice Hall of India, 1979.

Brower, R.A. *The Fields of Light: An Experiment in Critical Reading.* New York, 1951.

Brown, E.K. 'E.M. Forster and the Contemplative Novel', *University of Toronto Quarterly* III, April 1934.

—— 'Rhythm in Forster's "A Passage to India"', *Forster: A Collection of Critical Essays*, ed. Malcolm Bradbury. New Delhi: Prentice Hall of India, 1979.

Cecil, David. *Poets and Story Tellers: A Book of Critical Essays*. London: Macmillan, 1949.

Colmer, John. *A Passage to India*. London: Edward Arnold, 1967.

Crews, Frederick C. The Perils of Humanism—A Study of E.M. Forster. Princeton: Princeton University Press, 1961.

Dauner, Louise. 'What Happened in The Cave? Reflections on "A Passage to India"', Perspectives of E.M. Forster's 'A Passage to India', ed. V.A. Shahane. New York: Barucs, 1968.

Furbank, P.N. *E.M. Forster: A Life*, Vol. 2. London: Secker and Warburg, 1977.

Gransden, K.W. *E.M. Forster*. New York: Oliver and Boyd, 1962.

Kettle, Arnold. *An Introduction to the English Novel-II*. New Delhi: B.I. Publications, rpt. 1978.

Martin, John Sayre. *E.M. Forster: The Endless Journey*. New Delhi: Vikas Publishing House, 1976.

Moran, Jo Ann Hoeppner. 'E.M. Forster's "A Passage to India": What Really Happened in the Caves', *Modern Fiction Studies*, Vol. 34, No. 4, Winter, 1988.

Murry, Middleton. 'The Break Up of the Novel', 1924.

Parry, Benita. 'Passage to More than India', *Forster: A Collection of Critical Essays*, ed. Bradbury. New Delhi: Prentice Hall of India, 1979.

Shahane, V.A. *E.M. Forster: A Reassessment*. New Delhi: Kitab Mahal, 1962.

—— A *Passage to India: A Study*. New Delhi: Oxford University Press, 1977.

Stone, Wilfred. *The Cave and The Mountain: A Study of E.M. Forster*, Stanford: Stanford University Press, 1966.

Trilling, Lionel. *E.M. Forster—A Study*. London: The Hogarth Press, 1944.

Warren, Austin. 'E.M. Forster', *The American Review*, 1937.

White, Gertrude M. 'A Passage to India: Analysis and Revaluation', *PMLA*, LXVIII, September 1953.

Woolf, Virginia. 'The Novels of E.M. Forster', *Collected Essays*, Vol. I, London, 1966.

2

Quest for Human Harmony in Forster's *A Passage to India*

Sunita Sinha

A Passage to India is a rich, multilayered novel, highly complex in both form and argument and is indeed one of the most critically discussed novels within the canon. An elegant evocation of British India, *A Passage to India*, however, does not simply explore the path to a greater understanding of India, but explores man's quest for the ultimate truth. Forster found in India a vast physical and mental landscape to develop his themes; an 'objective correlative' for the forces against which all humanistic endeavour is pitted. The novel is deliberately and consciously polyphonic and symphonic in design, raising various perspectives and revealing Forster as an anti-imperialist, a humanist and a critic of Victorian middle class attitudes and colonial era racism. As a British colonialist in India himself, Forster saw first-hand the impossibility of friendship across racial divides, of the unification of India into a single nation and of the duration of British Raj. Like Conrad's *Heart of Darkness*, Forster's novel is a beautiful example of literature about the Empire, of sensitive literature at its best, studying the racial tensions and striving to explore the cultural clash but never sounding dogmatic.

What E.M. Forster offers in *A Passage to India* is a withering portrait of racism in British India, a portrait which inevitably draws comparison with Jean Renoir's, *The River*, which focuses on British expatriates living in India and Anthony Burgess's, *The Malayan Trilogy* in its evocation of the sights, the sounds, the colours and feelings of another country, respecting its 'otherness' at the same time. An extraordinary evocation of a land through alien eyes, Forster's India also ranks with Graham Greene's evocation of Mexico in *The Power and Glory* and with Conrad's portrayal of Africa in the *Heart of Darkness*. Both Conrad and Forster utilize Britain's Age of Empire as a backdrop for the narratives and they explore British attitudes and behaviour in the exotic locales of the imperial frontier. As Shirley Galloway rightly remarks—"*Heart of Darkness* and *A Passage to India* feature British characters who have internalized the ideological assumptions of their natural superiority to the Africans and Indians.... The characters in both the novels deal differently with the fundamental contradiction between systematic dehumanization for economic gain and the ideological justification of 'civilizing' the natives."[1]

The title of the novel is drawn from Walt Whitman's poem, 'Passage to India' as Forster himself has acknowledged. Just as the poem stresses the need to combine the successes of Western civilization with a new exploration of spiritual experiences and welcomes the opening of the Suez Canal as a step in this direction, so Forster's novel relates the ideas of human harmony to the secrets of the inner life and the mystery of the whole Universe. Both speak of a similar quest but whereas Whitman's poem celebrates the opening of the Suez Canal as bringing together East and West, *A Passage to India* begins and ends with the question—Can the English and Indian races be friends?—and, at the end of the novel the answer appears to be "No, not yet." Kipling's assertion, 'ne'er the twain shall meet' further qualifies it.

A useful comment from Martin Green, establishes the significance of Forster's work—"One could read all the works of the great tradition, and never know that England had an empire."[2] Forster's work raises issues of empire and race in ways which had never been attempted before. Kipling represented the East as a training ground for manliness, decency and character building. Forster, in contrast, challenged Kipling's perspective and brought his own perspective to the India question; and was deeply critical of the British position. But this is not a one-sided novel: it exposes uncomfortable truths regarding India as much as it does uncomfortable truths of Empire and oppression.

Examining the themes of class differences and hypocrisy in the early 20th century British society, *A Passage to India* is an admirable novel, which captures Forster's sense of awe at the kind of ageless wisdom and inexplicable phenomena to be encountered in India as well as the British tendency to dismiss it all as savage, rather than simply different. When *A Passage to India* appeared in 1924, many Anglo-Indians felt outraged at his evocation of a picture of society in India under the British Raj, of the clash between East and West and of the prejudices and misunderstandings that foredoomed goodwill. Forster's novel however admitted that his portrayal of Anglo-Indians was only slightly exaggerated. Through Ronnie Heaslop, the city magistrate, Forster expresses the views of the contemporary Anglo-Indians for whom the 'East' was a "career". Forster's novel satirizes such views of India as career or a training ground which are visible in various other novels about India like George Orwell's *Burmese Days* or *Shooting an Elephant*.

An anti-imperialist, Forster effectively brings out the relations between the colonizer and the colonized and his criticism of imperialism is liberal. He approaches the Anglo-Indian imperialism in terms of public school attitude: the prejudice, snobbery, priggishness, complacency, censoriousness and narrowmindedness. His works abound with highly satirical portraits of the English middle-class culture and point towards something deficient within the English national character. As Forster remarks—"For it is not that the Englishmen can't feel—it is that he is afraid to feel. He has been taught at his public school that feeling is bad form. He must not express great joy or sorrow, or even to open his mouth too wide when he talks—his pipe might fall out if he did. He must bottle up his emotions, or let them out only on a very special occasion."[3] Forster's portrait of the Raj is very convincing, as he was thoroughly familiar with the realities of the Raj. Having spent two years in India, in 1912 and again in 1921-22, he was closely involved in Indian affairs, supported Gandhi's Non Cooperation Movement of the early 1920's and remained a commentator in the inter-war period, hence his account of India is culturally and historically specific.

Orientalism, a significant work by Edward Said in 1978, brought the concept of the 'other' into focus and analysed how the Orient were habitually dominated by the West and reduced to being 'the other' in the sense of alien, inferior and non-Western—"The Orient is not only adjacent to source of it's civilization and languages, it's cultural contestant, and one of it's deepest and most recurring image of the 'other'."[4] Forster too, in his adulthood was inspired by Orientalism as the Italian Renaissance and Greek paganism had inspired him in his youth. Forster's novel portrays the imperialist agenda of the West to rule the 'barbaric Orient'; the 'other', the mysterious, the exotic, the erotic, the superstitious and the irrational.

In his searing indictment of Brahmin hypocrisy in writing against untouchability, Mulk Raj Anand has used many of his conversations with E.M. Forster—a novelist whom Anand looked up to because he felt that, 'this particular Englishman had leaned on the side of India.' Forster's views as a humanist may be aptly summed up in the epigraph to his other masterpiece—*Howards End*—"Only connect". It epitomizes Forster's ideal of achieving a harmony between the discordant elements within man himself and between man and the universe. It is about the need for the two parts of society—the intellectual and cultural and the commercial—to meet and understand each other. Forster writes not only about the need for society to be interlinked as a whole, but of the need of individuals to "connect the prose and passion", to link their rational and emotional sides. His open-minded and humanist view of life is seen in his novels in their focus on human relationships and the need for tolerance, sympathy and love between individual human beings from different parts of society and different cultures. He spoke in favour of tolerance in many areas of life, and he vigorously opposed censorship. In his non-fictional work, *What I Believe*, he asserts, "I do not believe in Belief. But this is an age of Faith, and there are so many militant creeds that, in self-defence, one has to formulate a creed of one's own. Tolerance, good temper and sympathy are no longer enough in a world where ignorance rules, and science, which ought to have ruled, plays the pimp. Tolerance, good temper and sympathy—they are what matter really, and if the human race is not to collapse they must come to the front before long."[5] The urge of bridging the difference between the East and the West and exploring the barriers of race, of class, of age and gender seems to be Forster's prime concern in *A Passage to India*. The humanist in Forster makes him insist on the need to connect and debate about how Anglo-Indian rule could be liberalized through the new attitude of courtesy and decency. The novel is all about the human race's attempts to find a more lasting home. This study of racial and romantic tensions is a work of sensitive literature at its best. His voice is "the voice of the humanist—one seriously committed to human values while refusing to take himself too seriously. Its tone is inquiring not dogmatic. It reflects a mind aware of the complexities confronting those who wish to live spiritually satisfying and morally responsible lives in a world that contrives increasingly against individual needs. Sensitively and often profoundly, Forster's fiction explores the problems such people encounter."[6] Forster's famous essay *Two Cheers for Democracy*, which was originally printed in 1938 in the New York nation, reflected his concern for individual liberty. He assumed liberal humanism not dogmatically but ironically, writing in unceremonious sentences and making gentle stabs at pomposity and hypocrisy—"if I had to choose between betraying my country and betraying my friend, I hope I should have the guts to betray my country".[7]

Throughout the novel, the barriers to interracial friendship in a colonial context are explored and personally experienced by the principal characters—Fielding and Aziz. Forster's emphasis is firmly placed on the realms of the personal and the individual, rather than the social and political. His sustained liberal humanist world-view is inherent in his insistence on personal experience, individual experience and the sanctity of the personal.

A Passage to India is a perfect combination of symbolic suggestion, psychological insight and social realism. Not many novelists have so successfully fused these elements as Forster has done. Forster's vision combines beautifully the symbolic suggestion in William Golding's works, the psychological study in Joyce's novels and the visionary symbolism in Lawrence and Proust's method of looking at a character in a subconscious way. The novel has a tripartite musical form—Mosque, Caves and Temple which constitute a triangle of forces which keeps the plot well balanced. "Three Blocks of Sound"—that is what *A Passage to India* consists of. Reduced to the barest terms, the structure of *A Passage to India* has the "rhythmic rise—fall— rise", that Forster found in what has been for him the greatest of novels, "War and Peace". The dialectical structure which consists of positive affirmation (Mosque), negative retraction (Caves), muted reaffirmations (Temple) is reflected in every detail.

The first part, 'Mosque', determines the background and unfolds the plot. The opening character does much more than to introduce us to the Indian city of Chandrapore. It establishes a striking contrast between the disordered chaotic life of the city and the rationally ordered but sterile life at the English civil station. The book's first passage the reader learns about, is that of Adela Quested and Mrs. Moore to visit Ronny Heaslop, who is the city magistrate. We are made acutely conscious of the deficiencies and the dull routine, the added meaningless ritual of life at the Civil Station through the disappointment and boredom of the two newcomers—Mrs. Moore, Ronny Heaslop's mother and Adela Quested his fiancée. The first key meeting of the novel is Mrs. Moore's encounter with the Muslim doctor, Aziz, the novel's Indian protagonist, at a Mosque by the Ganges. Mrs. Moore has been invested with a penumbra of symbolic suggestions. When Aziz and Mrs. Moore meet in the Mosque, both are seeking to escape from an alien environment. For Aziz, the beauty of the Mosque is a release from the Anglo-Indian incubus, for Mrs. Moore an escape from the pseudo-metropolitan atmosphere sedulously imitated by the paltry production of Cousin Kate. Aziz rages at her as the Englishwoman steps into the moonlight. But Mrs. Moore does the right thing—she removes her shoes—says the right thing—"God is here"[8]—and in a minute they are friends. "The flame that not even beauty can nourish", (24) was springing up in Aziz for this red faced woman. When she remarks,

"I do not think I understand people very well, I only know whether I like or dislike them" (24). Aziz declares, "Then you are an Oriental" (24). This moment of revelation—a muted epiphany—is the novel's positive affirmation. Nothing that happens later wholly invalidates the understanding achieved by these two dissimilar people. Forster includes a similar moment of intuitive understanding between Aziz and Ralph towards the end of the novel and the repeated motive—"Then you are an Oriental" recalls vividly for Aziz, and of course, for the reader, the memory of the exquisite moment in the Mosque.

With her wonderful openness to life and her capacity to accept people and events without prior rationalization, Mrs. Moore in her intuitive understanding of people transcends the limitation of liberal rationalism. After her return from the Mosque, as she is about to hang her cloak she notices that on the tip of the peg there is a wasp. Her voice floats out to swell the night's uneasiness. The ironical contrast between her response and that of the two missionaries who are wondering if a wasp is included in God's beneficence reveals that the spirit of religion is more alive in her than in institutional Christianity. Her intimacy with Aziz deepens further at the party arranged at the Government College by Fielding, the Principal, and this party stands in stark contrast to the Bridge party organised by Mr. Turton, the Collector of Chandrapore, which signalled the inevitable failure of all formal attempts to facilitate a better understanding between the two races. The volatile but likeable young Indian doctor, Aziz, invites them to a picnic at the Marabar Caves and thus, the next musical motif is introduced.

The slightly heightened style with which the section, 'Caves', opens declares unmistakably that the story has entered a new phase. The visions of harmony with which 'Mosque' ended are dispelled by the poetic evocations of primeval India. "The Marabar Caves are older than all spirits, pre-human, alien, indefinable" (124). In bringing his characters to the Caves, Forster is confronting them at a symbolic level with a part of India which eludes Western religion and philosophy of life. As the elephant carries them towards the Caves, there is a new quality in the landscape, a "spiritual silence which invaded more senses than the ear" (139). The "nullah" where Nawab Bahadur's accident occurred is linked with almost geographical accuracy to the very source of evil in the Marabar hills, the 'original spawning place' of the Caves and provides as it were, a channel through which evil flows towards Chandrapore.

L.C. Knights calls 'Macbeth' 'a statement of evil'; the section 'Caves' in *A Passage to India* constitutes Forster's statement of evil. It lends a metaphysical dimension to a novel that might otherwise have moved on a merely socio-political plane. To Frank Kermode, Forster is frankly a symbolist. Forster himself states, "my main purpose was not political, was not even sociological". One can start at the opening chapter— indeed the opening line—"Except for the Marabar Caves and they are twenty miles off, the city of Chandrapore presents nothing extraordinary" (1). Easy, colloquial, if with the touch of a guide book, the words set out a scene. But they will reach out and shape the organic whole.

Evil is externalized in the novel by the Marabar echo, the prelude to which, "pomper, pomper, pomper" is heard when the train crosses the first "nullah" on the way to Marabar. It is Forster's finest rhythm and is completely organic. There is not a hint of device in it. The echo which sounds, "bourn, oum, oum, oum" reverberates throughout the second part of the novel like an ominous clearly enunciated symphonic theme. It is an elaborate repetition of the metaphors of the goblin walking quietly over the universe in Beethoven's fifth symphony in *Howards End*. The goblin's message is that of panic and emptiness and always threatens the splendour of life. The Caves reiterate the same message of emptiness and nullity but more insistently and powerfully.

In the very first cave that Mrs. Moore visits she has a horrible experience. Besides, the crush and stench there is a terrifying echo in the cave. The echo murmurs—"Pathos, piety, courage, they exist but are identical and so is filth. Everything exists, nothing has value" (147). It is an utterly nihilistic vision. The echo has the effect of undermining and disintegrating Mrs. Moore's hold on life, and ultimately of destroying her. We are presented with a nightmare vision of evil and negation that is a challenge to Christianity and pretensions of the Western, liberal minds. Mrs. Moore has changed as a result of her experience at the Marabar Caves, she has become cynical and apathetic and indifferent to the world of personal relationships. "Why all this marriage? The human race would have become a single person centuries ago if marriage was any use" (197). Soon afterwards she leaves India as she crosses the country by train to go abroad. At Bombay she thinks, "I have not seen the right places", the voice of the Marabar Caves was not the voice of India, only one of the voices but it had prevented her from hearing the others, the voice of Asirgarh for instance, that is sighted from the train twice and seemed to say, I do not vanish—"So you thought an echo was India; you took the Marabar Caves as final? They laughed. What have we in common with them?" (205). In the passage home Mrs. Moore dies and her body is committed to the Indian Ocean. Mrs. Moore is resurrected again in the section Temple in the form of her two children Ralph and Stella.

The collision of the boats in which Ralph and Aziz, Stella and Fielding are watching the ceremony, is the final epiphany and brings harmony where a rational explanation has failed. One of the voices of India, that Mrs. Moore has not heard, has spoken with trenchant power—the voice of the Temple and strangely her own voice has spoken in unison with it. The symbolic structure requires that Adela, like Mrs. Moore should be confronted with the unknown; in Adela's case, the unknown is the universe within her own nature. Her experience is even more traumatic than Mrs. Moore's. The simplest interpretation of Adela's belief that she has been attacked by Aziz is to say that it is only an objectification of intense emotional assault on her reason that she has tried vainly to surpass. She has tried to live by the mind and is ashamed that animal desires have brought her and Ronny together. The imagined assault is a reflection of her deeply divided being, of the unresolved battles of forces, within her, and also of her lack of self-knowledge. We may think of the entry into the Caves as perhaps representing a descent into the subconscious. Everything Adela stands for—British common sense, repression of emotions, instinct for compromise is wrought up against an over-whelming force with which it cannot come to terms. F.S. Crews gives a more blunt interpretation that Adela is physically attracted to Aziz and subconsciously desires to be raped by him. The incident provokes the sharpest conflict between East and West—Aziz is immediately placed under arrest. The Anglo-Indian community in India is thoroughly amused. Aziz's friends are equally stirred. Reason is thrown to the winds by both sides, and only Fielding keeps proportion.

The last section is a muted epiphany and a partial reconciliation of the major discords of the novel. In the Caves, love is denied and life declared to be sterile, in the Temple love is born and life confirmed. We have escaped in time and space from the Marabar Hills and all they symbolize, and are promised an apotheosis, a rending of the veil and an imaginative transfiguration. There are three crucial intimations of perfect harmony. First Godbole's vision when he impels the image of Mrs. Moore and wasp into his consciousness and achieves liberation from selfhood. We see Godbole standing in the presence of "God" during a Hindu birth ceremony. Godbole's sudden remembrance of Mrs. Moore is an odd intrusion into the specifically Hindu ceremony, but not entirely inappropriate. The only English character in the novel that can effortlessly interact with the Indian culture, Mrs. Moore, stands in opposition to Fielding, whose independence and pragmatism make him unsuitable to both Eastern and Western culture. Forster juxtaposes the

Hindu birth ceremony that culminates in 'The Temple' with the rebirth of Dr. Aziz of the first few chapters.

It is the collision of the boats that brings into sudden symbolic focus and fine reconciliation, the antagonist forces in the novel. The plunging of characters into the water tank suggests a form of spiritual baptism, a form of purification. The sources of misunderstanding are scattered on the waters. The rain suggests the release of the forces of imaginative love. The collision of the boats forms the climax of *A Passage to India*, providing a sharp confrontation between Aziz and Fielding, between the East and the West. It is an ironic event, because the reconciliation between Aziz and Fielding occurs after a comic mishap. But Forster is too honest a novelist to fake a happy ending by suggesting that the reconciliation will last. The last paragraph of the novel describing the last ride together of Aziz and Fielding and ending in the words, "No, not yet,"—"No, not there," (317) epitomises the oscillations between affirmation and retraction, vision and anti-vision, that have characterized the novel.

Forster ends *A Passage to India* with a bitter sweet reconciliation between Aziz and Fielding but also with the realization that the two cannot be friends under the contemporary conditions. Thus, Forster ends the novel as a tragic but platonic love story between the two friends, separated by different cultures and political climates. Forster does not express any definitive political standpoint on the sovereignty of India. Fielding suggests that British rule over India, if relinquished, would be replaced by a different sovereign that would be perhaps worse than the English. Aziz, however, does make the point that it is British rule in India that prevents the two men from remaining friends, Forster, thus, indicates that British rule in India creates significant problems for the country and is unable to offer an easy or concrete solution to these problems.

As John Colmer beautifully sums up—"The final effect is not one of pessimism, but of qualified optimism, since we witness a variety of approaches to truth, each having something in common with the other, each having a relative validity, none being complete.... The moral and imaginative effect of the novel is to make us more sensitive to the importance of love and imagination in human affairs, to make us skeptical of putting our trust in any one religion or creed and to believe in the unique power of beauty and personal relations."[9]

NOTES

1. Galloway Shirley, in an article on Forster.
2. Green Martin, comments in an article on Forster.
3. E.M. Forster, in a 1921 article, "Notes on the English Character".
4. Edward Said, *Orientalism* (London, Penguin Books, 1985).
5. E.M. Forster, in his famous essay, "What I Believe".
6. Quoted in a series on British Authors (Cambridge University Press).
7. E.M. Forster, in his famous essay, "Two Cheers for Democracy".
8. E.M. Forster, *A Passage to India*. All quotations in this article from *A Passage to India* have been taken from the edition published in 2006 (New Delhi: AITBS Publishers).
9. John Colmer and E.M. Forster, *A Passage to India* (Edward Arnold Publishers Ltd., 1969).

3

A Passage to India as Modernist Narrative: A Study

Sreemati Mukherjee

A Passage to India, written within the overarching assumptions of realism, is punctuated with and interrogated by a discourse of symbolism that gives the narrative the kind of incalculability that is suggested by its central image or leitmotif, the Marabar Caves. As much as the novel advances the idea of a story, it admits its own inscrutability and impenetrability, perhaps through the frequent invocations to Night, which bathe the events of the novel in a certain murkiness, gloom and opacity. If the language of the novel obeys the nineteenth century premise of referentiality, its frequent invocation of "night" suggests exactly the opposite, the lack of referentiality or transparency.

The word "passage" of the title opens up the manifold implications associated with it, suggesting that the novel's thematic concern is perhaps, a rite of passage, a journey, a discovery or a quest. Indeed, the quest implications of the plot are realized in the somewhat unusual name of the heroine, Adela Quested, who has made this "passage" not only to find fulfilment in love, but also to know the "real" India. Adela's journey takes on the nature of a heroic quest, where her "passage" to the real India, takes her into a terrifying darkness at the heart of life, somewhat analogous to the "heart of darkness" in Conrad's Congo interior.[1]

The darkness of Forster's modernist vision, however, involves heroic action. Adela, the woman who is one of the most important narrative centers of the text, persistently queries as to where the "truth" of life lies. As she asks her friend and companion, Mrs. Moore, "...Mrs. Moore, if one isn't absolutely honest, what is the use of existing?" (105). Indeed, her "passage" to India tests the ultimate limits of her integrity as a person which surfaces in the enigmatic narrator's comments on Adela's heroic trial of action and endurance, "...she was no longer examining life, but being examined by it; she had become a real person" (272). When the impersonal narrator, who is otherwise closely involved in the aesthetics of gloom and pessimism that the text generates, describes Adela's moment of heroic enterprise, his admiration for her comes through in the use of words like "armour" and "splendour" which raise echoes of epic action and epic deeds:

> A new and unknown sensation protected her like invisible armour.... The fatal day recurred, in every detail, but now she was of it and not of it at the same time, and this double relation gave it indescribable splendour. (253)

The text also valorizes Fielding's spirited and loyal defence of his Indian friend, Aziz, and his resolute break with his own community in order to do it. Thus, even though, the echo in the Marabar Caves enunciates that "Pathos, piety, courage—they exist, but are identical, and so is filth. Everything exists, but nothing has value" (165), the novel still asserts the value of human action in the face of life's ability to turn all meaning into chaos. This concern for meaning is also reflected in the novel's formal structure, which follows a kind of Aristotelian plot progression with exposition (beginning), complication (middle) and denouement (end), and the pivotal nodes of tragic action, *anagnorisis* and *peripeteia*.[2]

Anagnorisis (recognition) and *peripeteia* (reversal), generate the peculiarly compelling dramatic aesthetics associated with tragic action. In that respect, like Tolstoy's *Anna Karenina* and Dostoevsky's *Crime and Punishment*, the action of *A Passage to India* involves a mistake and its tragic reversal. In the process, an entire society, that of British India and its multi-tiered social structure, is revealed with many moments of comic irony and satire and the varied characterization of "round" and "flat"[3] characters, the treatment of comic figures, as some critics have pointed out, specially reminiscent of Jane Austen.[4] However, underneath this polite façade of civilization, Forster alludes to an untamed and potentially disruptive psyche that has the power to rent the social fabric apart with the violence of an animal.

Like the modernist aesthetics that surface in novels by Joyce, Woolf and Faulkner, Forster, in spite of his chiseled and formally symmetrical plot, alludes to and gears his thematics and poetics around the central fact of interiority as artistic method. The aesthetics of the interior surfaced as early as Romantic poetry, memorably in works like Coleridge's *The*

Rime of the Ancient Mariner and Byron's *Manfred*. However, interiority becomes a philosophy of narrative in the modern novel, whose leading theorist Virginia Woolf, taking issue with the "materialism" of Bennet, Wells and Galsworthy in the essay "Modern Fiction", puts it in the following manner:[5]

> Life is not a series of gig lamps symmetrically arranged; life is a luminous halo, a semi-transparent envelope surrounding us from the beginning of consciousness to the end.[6]

In the same essay she further adds,

> Let us record the atoms as they fall upon the mind in the order in which they fall, let us trace the pattern, however disconnected or incoherent in appearance, which each sight or incident scores upon the consciousness. Let us not take it for granted that life exists more fully in what is commonly thought big than in what is commonly thought small.[7]

Let us note Forster's convergences and divergences from Woolf's position. Clearly, he is not an advocate of the apparent formlessness warranted by the "disconnected" and "incoherent" atoms of thought and experience, often called the *"monologue interieur"*[8] or "interior monologue" that conditions the novels of Joyce, Faulkner and Woolf. The formal perfection of Forster's novel puts him in the same league as the masters of tragic plot construction who exploit the fatal implications of recognition and reversal, so that the tragic irony of human existence can be realized to the fullest extent. However, it is with regard to the primacy of interiority in his novel and his ordering of his central symbol or leitmotif that Forster clearly locates himself within a modernist aesthetic practice.

Like Virginia Woolf's use of the "lighthouse" in the novel of the same name and Faulkner's use of the scent of the magnolia in *Sound and Fury*, Forster uses leitmotif, an artistic tactic that many modernists have borrowed from Wagner,[9] to underscore and heighten their central concerns in their respective novels, which enact a tense dialectic between form and formlessness, between chaos and meaning. As Peter Burra claims in his introduction to the 1957 Everyman edition of *A Passage to India*, "The leitmotif need not in itself be peculiarly significant, but by association with its previous appearance accumulates meaning each time it recurs."[10] The central leitmotif in Forster's text, carrying the implications of the text beyond the merely visible, apprehensible, rationally and spatially ordered universe, raising questions about art, history, time and space, are the Marabar Caves, which are introduced very early in the text, and to which the text comes back with an almost compulsive, artistic and psychological insistence. This is how Burra sums up the role of the Marabar Caves as leitmotif: "...the 'Marabar caves' are the basis of a *tour de force* in literary planning. They are the keynote in the symphony to which the strange melody always returns."[11]

Let us analyse the significance of the terms "melody" and "symphony" in Forster's poetics as a whole. In this context, it is important to remind ourselves that Forster was a musician and that he emphasized the need to express the generic dimensions of music into the modern novel: "Yes,—oh dear yes—the novel tells a story...and I wish that it was not so, that it could be something different—melody, or perception of the truth, not this low atavistic form."[12] There is melody in a Forster novel, his own adaptation of the Wagnerian leitmotif, and what he possibly calls "Rhythm" in his chapter "Pattern and Rhythm" (137) in *Aspects of the Novel*.[13]

In Burra's words, "In *A Passage to India*, one of the most 'aesthetically compact' books ever written whose thought, like music's cannot be fixed, nor its meaning defined, there is an extreme instance of one passage calling back to other"[14] (xviii). As Burra emphasizes, "Mosque, Caves, Temple" are planned like symphonies in three movements that are given their shape and their inter-connection by related and contrasted localities"[15] (xix).

Let us now look at Forster's introduction of the Marabar Caves whose presence is prepared for from the opening line of the novel, and which end the first chapter of the novel, with these words, "These fists and fingers are the Marabar Hills, containing the extraordinary caves" (6). Describing the Dravidian hills where the Marabar Caves are situated, the narrator exclaims:

> There is something unspeakable in these outposts. They are like nothing else in the world, and a glimpse of them makes the breath catch. They rise abruptly, insanely, without the proportion that is kept by the wildest hills elsewhere, they bear no relation to anything dreamt or seen. To call them "uncanny" suggests ghosts, and they are older than all spirit. Hinduism has scratched and plastered a few rocks, but the shrines remain unfrequented...even Buddha,

> who must have passed this way down to the Bo Tree of
> Gya, shunned a renunciation more complete than his
> own, and has left no legend of struggle or victory in the
> Marabar. (136)

The "uncanny" is a significant dimension of the aesthetics that the novel offers, this too, an offshoot of the preoccupation with the bizarre, the fantastic and the aberrant that Romanticism as a movement engaged in. Other symbols or leitmotifs that the text introduces to gather and concentrate its meaning, are the frequent invocations of night, the presence of animal agents threateningly close to human activity and feeling, the monstrous heat, the tropical sun, the serpent, the wasp and the worm." The leitmotifs by constantly recalling each other set up possibilities of both irony (through contrast) and symbolism. In Burra's words, "This device—of motifs, irony, and symbols—is, in fact, the modern equivalent of the classical unities, an invention of the greatest value, having all the classical advantages and none of their so severe limitations"[16] (xix).

As Melvin Friedman asserts in "The Symbolist Novel", it is in the use of leitmotifs or symbols that modernist narrative interrogates the generic boundaries between fiction and poetry,[17] making fiction do more and more the task of poetry, which is using valorizing the subjective and the intuitive as significant modes of organizing both time and space. Not only the psychologizing of the novel, but the poeticizing of the novel, is a radical feature of modernist narrative. This mixing, cross-examining and interchange of genres, becomes yet another feature of an endlessly plural and radically experimental modernist aesthetic practice

Coming first to the question of locale in which the novel is set, Chandrapore is incurably ugly and dirty, divesting the traditional romantic locale of all its glamour, mystery and mythical splendour. If anything, it enacts the debunking of myth. As the narrator wryly comments at the very outset of the novel,

> So abased, so monotonous is everything that meets
> the eye, that when the Ganges comes down it might be
> expected to wash the excrescence back into the soil. (4)

This unromantic locale is also marred by the presence of excessive heat and a ferocious sun. One can also sense the subjective ordering of time and place in the novel, what in fact, I would, in following Peter Brooks, call the narrative "desire" of the novel.[18] In describing the petulance exhibited by most people at Fielding's tea party, the narrator says, "It was as if irritation oozed from the very soil" (83). The narrator ascribes real personality and energy to the heat, when, in describing the unpleasant onset of the hot season, he says, "The heat had leapt forward in the last hour..." (123). His development of the leitmotif of heat underscores the poetry in his method, which like musical repetition and recurrence, holds a composition together:

> It was early in the morning, for the day, as the hot weather advanced, swelled like a monster at both ends and left less and less room for the movements of mortals. (219)

Again, the narrator adds a few pages later,

> Making sudden changes of gear, the heat accelerated its advance after Mrs. Moore's departure until existence had to be endured and crime punished with the thermometer at a hundred and twelve. (233)

Describing the onset of April, the narrator raising echoes of the April leitmotif in Eliot's *The Waste Land*, says,[19]

> April, herald of horrors, is at hand. The sun was returning to his kingdom with power but without beauty— that was the sinister feature.... He was not the unattainable friend, either of men or birds or other suns, he was not the eternal promise, ...he was merely a creature, like the rest, and so debarred from glory. (124)

This bestializing of the world is particularly evident in the frequency with which animal images extend the implications of the human world, or cast a sinister shadow over human affairs. At the same moment that Adela Quested and Ronny Heaslop find some togetherness and resonance in the touching of their hands their mood of harmony is disturbed by the presence of a hyena which accidentally hits the fender of their car (94-96). This proximity of the animal world to the human, constantly interrogates the sanctities and pleasures of the human. At the entrance to the Marabar Caves, Adela thinks she has seen a snake, which Aziz dismisses as a rope (155). There is some confusion over whether the object is a snake or a rope, a classic example of error in Vedantic non-dualism which holds Maya responsible for causing error or ignorance and thereby causing suffering.[20]

The snake is a fairly ubiquitous symbol in the text, perhaps, once again, reflecting a narrative "desire" to engage with the snake symbol as pivotal to the meaning of life. Inside the Marabar Caves, once again, there are references to snakes created by lighting a match:

> Even the striking of a match starts a little worm coiling, which is too small to complete a circle but is eternally watchful. And if several people talk at once, an overlapping howling noise begins, echoes generate echoes, and the cave is stuffed with a snake composed of small snakes, which writhe independently. (163)

One can see how the grotesque and a plunging of the text into disturbing images that suggest the uncanny and gesture towards the irrational ordering of time and space set the tone of the novel. The proliferation of the bestial is bound to suggest the irrational as a strong undercurrent, or as a major preoccupation in the work. The repetition and the recurrence of the snake image suggests a "desire" in the narrative to dwell in the dark and sinister regions of the psyche, where the border between the rational and the irrational is a very tenuous one, and the universe is perceived as threatening. Later, there are references to the venomous "Russel's viper" (194) found loose in Fielding's college. Ultimately, the jubilant crowd celebrating Aziz's vindication is described in the following manner:

> Like a snake in a drain, it advanced down the narrow bazaar towards the basin of the Maidan, where it would turn about itself, and decide on its prey. (261)

Another instance of the grotesque in the text is that soon after the accident with the hyena, the Nawab Bahadur, who was also in the car, narrates to a group of his fellow men, how a man who he had accidentally overrun years back, still remains to haunt him in an "unspeakable form" (107), close to the scene of his death. The borders between the rational and the irrational are constantly tested, to suggest the tenuousness of the rational ordering of experience. Helping to keep the tone of the novel biased in favour of the non-rational or irrational as a salient factor of experience is the presence of night as leitmotif. The references to night in the text are numerous. After the accident with the hyena, the narrator notes, "Never tranquil, never perfectly dark, the night wore itself away..." (107). The inscrutability that lies at the heart of this novel, is underscored through the inscrutable Indian Godbole, who is described as being "Ancient Night" (81).

Yet, the text tries to encompass the bestial with the human, the incalculable with the rational, night with light, by linking two human characters with the image of the wasp.

On her first night in Ronny's quarters Mrs. Moore finds a wasp:

> Going to hang up her cloak, she found that the tip of the peg was occupied by a small wasp.... Perhaps he mistook the peg for a branch—no Indian animal has any sense of an interior. Bats, rats, birds, insects will as soon nest inside a house as out; it is to them a normal growth of the *eternal jungle* (italics mine), which alternately produces houses trees, houses trees. (34)

It is funny that Godbole, who is the most inscrutable character in the novel, ostensibly devotional, but also called "Ancient Night" (81) and who possibly knew the meaning of the "terrifying echo" (162), heard by Mrs. Moore in the Marabar Caves, feels linked to Mrs. Moore through the wasp. During the Gokul Ashtami celebrations of Krishna's birthday, where too there is a reference to a cobra of papier mache (323), Godbole, singing and dancing, suddenly remembers both Mrs. Moore and the wasp:

> Thus Godbole, though she was not important to him remembered an old woman he had met in Chandrapore days...he impelled her by his spiritual force to that place where completeness can be found. Completeness not reconstruction. His senses grew thinner, her remembered a wasp seen he forgot where, perhaps on a stone. He loved the wasp equally, he impelled it likewise, he was imitating God.... (321)

What are the implications of Godbole's feelings or psychological and spiritual effort? The thrust of his expansive thoughts seems to be that we must embrace both the evil and the good in the world, and that God is in both. This is the central fact of Hinduism, of Vaishnavism, where God is love, and therefore evil is also love of self, and that the self is implicated in everything. In that respect, I would say that *A Passage to India*, tries to encompass the darkness of evil as a central fact of life. However, it is not able to balance this vision with an opposing thrust on beauty and goodness, although these elements as artistic form and human action are also present in the text.

Carrying the central thrust of the novel's philosophical implications is the vision of Mrs. Moore, as it relates to the Marabar Caves:

> —in the twilight of the double vision, a spiritual muddledom is set up for which no high sounding words can be found; we can neither act nor refrain from action, we can neither ignore nor respect infinity....
>
> What had spoken to her in that scoured out cavity of the granite? What dwelt in the first of the caves? Something very old and very small. Before time, it was before space also. Something snub-nosed, incapable of generosity— the undying worm itself. (231)

However, there is also a discourse of sensuousness and beauty in the text, an assertion of form and meaning over chaos and meaninglessness. One such moment is when Fielding, the cultivated and rational European gentleman, finds the meaning of life in Italian architecture. It is to be noted in this context that Fielding did not have the experience of either the surreal snakes or the "echo" in the Marabar Caves. In Venice, Fielding finds the true harmony between form and meaning, body and spirit:

> ...the harmony between the works of man and the earth that upholds them, the civilization that has escaped muddle, the spirit in a reasonable form with flesh and blood subsisting.... Writing picture post-cards to his Indian friends, he felt that they would miss the joys he experienced now, the joys of form.... The Mediterranean is the human norm. (314)

This is the discourse of rationality and the aesthetics of form, indirectly an assertion of European ideals, that the novel both upholds and debunks from time to time. The novel, as I have said before, performs a tense dialectic between form and formlessness, chaos and meaning, narrative "desire" being with either position at particular times, creating also the rich ambiguity that is also one of Modernism's prime effects affect in art.

The text also problematizes knowledge and language, which is the prime mode of human communication, once again reflecting modernist ethical, epistemological and aesthetic concerns. It never becomes quite clear what really happened to Adela Quested in the Marabar Caves, where she claimed to have been assaulted by the young Indian protagonist of the story, Dr. Aziz. At the end of *Oedipus Rex* or the *Oresteia*, we not only have definite knowledge about why the tragic incidents took place in the way they did, we also arrive at a moment of calm resignation in the face of life's vicissitudes memorably summed up at the end of *Samson Agonistes* as "And calm of mind, all passion spent."[21]

However, at the end of *A Passage to India*, not only do we not get to know what happened to Adela Quested in the Marabar Caves, but we also do not arrive at that *still* point of recognition and understanding that is not only aesthetically satisfying, but also lends us that equipoise with which to regard life with awe, reverence and calm.[22] Was it a "hallucination" on Adela's part, a kind of wish fulfilment as she herself puts it, "you suggest that I had an hallucination there, the sort of thing—though in an awful form—that makes some women think they've had an offer of marriage when none was made" (267). The text goes to elaborate lengths to link Adela's fears and anxieties about her own sexuality and impending marriage with Ronny Heaslop, and the incident at Marabar, with images of animals, bestiality and the irrational, thereby positing the bestial as a part of the human psyche and of the psyche as unknown and terrifying. This is the psychological subtext of the novel, which once again puts it in correlation to other modernist texts which explore the multiple and frightening dimensions of the psyche.

The darkness in the Caves can be seen as analogous to the unknown quality of the mind and its frightening mystery. The mystery at the heart of the text raises echoes of other mysteries faced and solved by mythical heroes like Oedipus, a mystery which can destroy you. Through the centrality of Adela Quested's "hallucination" (267), and the predominance of the "echo" that haunts and taunts both Adela and Mrs. Moore, the text offers us the possibility of a reality that is surreal and clearly beyond the borders of reason. It testifies to a frightening aesthetics of interiority that had been present in literature from the time of the romantics to surface as a narrative principle only in the modern period. We must also keep in mind that the darkness that overpowers the text may also have something to do with its European background, which had recently gone through the cataclysmic First World War. The book was published in 1924, and Forster served in Egypt during the war.

Like Joyce and Faulkner, Forster also problematizes language, revealing to us the possibility for corruption that lies at the heart of the primary medium of human communication. A startling example in the text which, though carrying comic dimensions, is nonetheless frightening in the incantatory quality it acquires when Mrs. Moore is transformed into "Esmiss Esmoor" which the crowd chants when it feels that its chief witness has been taken away from them. Somehow, "Esmiss Esmoor" in the fervour of its intensity and its deification of a human being, becomes conflated with another chant to which the crowd at the Gokul Ashtami festival sways with divine ecstasy, that chant which brings the novel to a point of closure:

> Tukaram, Tukaram,
> Thou art my father and mother and everybody.
> Tukaram, Tukaram,
> Thou art my father and mother and everybody.
> Tukaram, Tukaram

Tukaram was a saint and Mrs. Moore was almost given the status of a saint by the Indians at the trial, Forster treating with irony in both instances, the Indian tendency to deify human personalities. Although, Forster certainly makes the irrational an important epistemological category in the text, yet in the primacy that Fielding, the rational European gentleman, enjoys in the text, the discourse of reason is never really dismissed. Within such a framework, the text perhaps treats with delicate and sometimes obvious irony the tendency towards deification in the Indian sensibility. With reference to the hymn quoted above, the narrator says,

> They sang not even to the God who confronted them, but to a saint; they did not one thing which the non Hindu would feel dramatically correct; this approaching triumph of India was a muddle (as we call it), a frustration of reason and form. (319)

India emerges as a trope in the text of this muddle and mess which the narrator or Forster himself sees at the heart of life. Reinforcing his reading of life as a muddle, and the repeated challenges thrown to reason and justice is the comic corruption of words and the maddening diversifying and splitting of language into signification and lack of significance. Another droll and comic instance of the possibilities of transformation in language to produce bathos instead of elevation is the transformation of the words "God Is Love" into "God si Love" because of the error made by the draughtsman who had written these words for the Gokul Ashtami celebrations. In a way, in the breaking and comic debunking of language, Forster is not only in the company of Joyce, but also foreshadows Samuel Beckett, who in a work like *Waiting For Godot*, reveals how easily the most elevated discourse or language can be made dysfunctional or ludicrous.

Thus, as I have said earlier, the novel both assents to and denies civilization, carrying out both a "dialogue"[23] and a dialectic between the opposing possibilities of assent and negation as psychological, artistic and even cosmic principles. The reality of evil, for instance, is alluded to many times in the text. As Fielding thinks: "...the evil was propagating in every direction, it seemed to have an existence of its own, apart from anything that was done or said by individuals..." (207-08). And yet, although, Fielding does not believe in Heaven, he believes "...honesty gets us there" (267).

Although, Forster affirms and asserts storytelling as a principle in the novel as a genre, he also alludes to its possibilities for generic transformation and mutation in introducing and imbibing techniques from music, which he calls the "melody" of a work. In this respect, he is closely allied with the radical experimentation with form that marks Modernism as a movement, causing endless and mutual cross generic exchange, which not only makes genre very pluralistic, but also reveals in its own way, the artist's interrogation of tradition and history. In Forster's emphasis on chaos as more preeminent than design and order, and the irrational, the hallucinatory, the simulacrum as constantly interposing and juxtaposing itself to any rational order of things, Forster interrogates Time and Space themselves, the two most important coordinates of the novel as a genre. Thus, the novel performs a rich ambiguity of both assenting to art and calling it into question, of affirming the novel as a genre, and cross-examining it from within to give it a fascinating multiplicity and paradoxical quality.

NOTES

1. Refer to Joseph Conrad's *Heart of Darkness and The Secret Sharer*. Toronto and New York: Bantam Books, 1981.
2. "Anagnorisis (Greek discovery) refers to the startling discovery that suddenly leads the protagonist to a changed state of affairs—from ignorance to knowledge and the entire scheme of things requires readjustment of a kind never conceived of previously. It is discussed by Aristotle in his *Poetics* as an essential part of the plot of a tragedy, although anagnorisis occurs in comedy, epic and, at a later date, the novel as well. This kind of recognition is artistically more satisfying because it is accompanied by a peripeteia, the shift in fortune from good to bad that moves on to the tragic catastrophe." Refer I.H-Shihan. *Literary and Critical Terms*. Delhi: Imprint, 2005, 5-6.

3. E.M. Forster, *Aspects of the Novel*. London: Edward Arnold Publishers, 1927, 65.

4. Lionel Trilling, *E.M. Forster*. Uniform Edition. Oxford. Melbourne: Oxford University Press, 1982.

5. Virginia Woolf, "Modern Fiction." *The Common Reader*. First Series. Ed. Andrew McNeillie. New York and London: A Harvest Book, Harcourt, Inc. 1925, 150.

6. *Ibid.*

7. *Ibid.*

8. For the term "monologue interieur" see Melvin J. Friedman. "The Symbolist Novel." *Modernism*. Ed. Malcolm Bradbury and James Mcfarlane. London: Penguin Books, 1991, 455.

9. *Ibid.*, 453-54.

10. E.M. Forster, *A Passage to India*. Ed. Peter Burra. London: J.M. Dent & Sons, Ltd., 1957, xvii.

11. *Ibid.*, xix.

12. E.M. Forster, *Aspects of the Novel*. London: Edward Arnold, 1927, 27.

13. *Ibid.*, 137-55.

14. E.M. Forster, *A Passage to India*. Ed. Peter Burra. London: J.M. Dent & Sons, Ltd., 1957, xviii.

15. *Ibid.*, xix.

16. *Ibid.*

17. Melvin J. Friedman, "The Symbolist Novel." *Modernism*. Ed. Malcolm Bradbury and James Mcfarlane. London: Penguin Books, 1991.

18. "Desire" as Peter Brooks analyses it in his psychoanalytical reading of narrative, is the leading emotion that surfaces in a novel in which the reader too is implicated. See "Narrative Desire" in Peter Brooks, *Reading For The Plot*. Cambridge, Massachusetts: Harvard University Press, 1992, 37-61.

19. Refer "April is the cruelest month... " in T.S. Eliot's *The Waste Land. The Complete Poems and Plays*, 1909-1950. New York: HBJ Publishers, 1950, 37.

20. For an elaborate analysis of the rope/snake illusionary dilemma, see "The Philosophy of Shankara" in *The Cultural Heritage of India*, Volume III, Ramakrishna Institute of Culture: Calcutta, 1953, 240-42.

21.   Milton, *Samson Agonistes* in *Milton Poetical Works*. Ed. Douglas Bush. Oxford and New York: Oxford University Press, 1969, 558.

22.   For the notion of the "still point," see T.S. Eliot. *Murder In The Cathedral. The Complete Poems and Plays*, 1909-1950. New York: HBJ Publishers, 1950, 182.

23.   For the idea of "dialogue" in the novel, see M.M. Bakhtin, *The Dialogic Imagination*. Trans. Caryl Emerson and Michael Holquist. Austin: University of Texas Press, 1981,12.

WORKS CITED

Primary Source

Forster, E.M. *A Passage to India*. San Diego, New York and London: A Harvest Book. Harcoutt Brace & Company, 1924. All page references are from this book.

Secondary Sources

Aeschylus. *The Oresteian Trilogy*. Trans. Philip Vellacott. Middlesex and New York: Penguin Books, 1956.

Bakhtin, M.M. *The Dialogic Imagination*. Trans. Caryl Emerson and Michael Holquist. Austin: University of Texas Press, 1981.

Beckett, Samuel. *Waiting For Godot in The Complete Dramatic Works*. London: Faber & Faber, 1956.

Bhattacharya, Surendranath. "The Philosophy of Shankara." *The Cultural Heritage of India*. Volume III. Ramakrishna Institute of Culture, Calcutta, 1953.

Brooks, Peter. *Reading For The Plot*. Cambridge and Massachusetts: Harvard University Press, 1992.

Byron, Lord. *Manfred. Byron's Poetry*. Ed. Frank D. Mcconnell. New York and London: W.W. Norton & Company, 1978, 124-59.

Coleridge, Samuel T. *The Rime of the Ancient Mariner. The Norton Anthology*. Vol. 2. Sixth edition. General Editor: M.H. Abrams. New York and London: W.W. Norton & Company, 1993.

Dostoevsky, Fyodor. *Crime and Punishment*. Trans. David Magarshack. New York: Penguin Books, 1951.

Eliot, T.S. *The Waste Land* in *The Complete Poems and Plays*, 1909-1950. New York: HBJ Publishers, 1950.

——— *Murder In The Cathedral* in *The Complete Poems and Plays*, 1909-1950. New York: HBJ Publishers, 1950.

Friedman, Melvin J. "The Symbolist Novel." *Modernism.* Ed. Malcolm Bradbury and James Mcfarlane. London: Penguin Books, 1991.

Forster, E.M. *Aspects of the Novel.* London: Edward Arnold Publishers, 1927.

—— *A Passage to India.* Ed. Peter Burra. London: J.M. Dent & Sons, Ltd., 1957.

H-Shihan, I. *Literary and Critical Terms.* Delhi: Imprint, 2005.

Milton, John. *Samson Agonistes in Poetical Works.* Ed. Douglas Bush. Oxford and New York: Oxford University Press, 1969.

Sophocles. *King Oedipus* in *The Theban Plays.* Trans. E.P. Watling. New York: Penguin Books, 1947.

Trilling, Lionel. *E.M. Forster.* Uniform Edition. Oxford and Melbourne: Oxford University Press, 1982.

Tolstoy, Leo. Anna Karenina. Trans. David Magarshack. New York: A Signet Classic, 1961.

Woolf, Virginia. "Modern Fiction." *The Common Reader.* First Series. Ed. Andrew McNeillie. New York and London: A Harvest Book, Harcourt, Inc., 1925.

4

Gender, Race and Sexuality: Shifting Otherness in E.M. Forster's *A Passage to India*

Shikha Misra

When *A Passage to India* first appeared in 1924 in England it was criticised for being anti British and unreasonably biased. These views were soon to be replaced by fulsome praise, the novel being seen as a generous appreciation of the people of one race by the writer of another. Proclaimed a masterpiece *A Passage to India* has been privileged over almost all other British fiction written about India. Western critics have placed a great deal of trust in Forster's vision of India. John Beer, in his introduction to G.K. Das's *E.M. Forster's India*, declares that the book was instrumental in the final cession of English power in India "revealing to many politicians in England the shaky kinds of foundation on which that power had been built, and the need for a graceful retreat".[1] Trilling on the other hand sees it as a book "not about India alone; it is about all of human life".[2]

The postcolonial theorist Abdul R. Jan Mohamed has posited two kinds of colonialist writing—the 'imaginary' and the 'symbolic'. In the 'imaginary' text, the emotive as well as the cognitive intentionalities are structured by 'objectification and aggression' accompanied by adamant refusal to admit the possibility of a rapprochement between Self and Other. 'Symbolic' texts, asserts Jan Mohamed citing Forster's *A Passage to India*, "attempt to find syncretic solutions to the Manichean opposition of the colonizer and the colonized", offering "the most interesting attempts to overcome the barriers of racial difference".[3]

The politics of such criticism has been debated in recent times, Forster's 'generous vision' has been seen as not so generous: this seemingly sympathetic text is unable to encounter the other without undermining that other—whether an it or him or her.

The story of the novel is told in three parts—*Mosque, Caves* and *Temple* and revolves around Aziz, a young Muslim doctor friendly to the British; Mrs. Moore, Ronny the City Magistrate's mother; Adela Quested, Ronny's fianceé—the two women but recently arrived from England; and Mr. Fielding, the government school teacher. Aziz organizes a picnic for the newcomers (Miss Quested wants to see the 'real India') to the famous Caves of Marabar. Adela Quested's experience in the caves leads to a charge of rape against Aziz. The reader never learns what if anything happened there (something 'unspeakable' says Forster).[4] The charge is never given a name, only referred to as an 'insult' in the English community. A face off between the two races is averted at the last moment when Adela retracts her accusation of Aziz.

At the centre of the novel, therefore, where there should have been a naming of the crime and the criminal there exists only a gap, an elision. Into this gap critics, prompted by Forster's statement that "in the cave it is *either* a man, *or* the supernatural or an illusion",[5] have rushed in with imaginatively reconstructed psychological exegesis. Just before entering the cave Adela, repressed, priggish and quite charmless ("not beautiful" is Aziz's verdict. "She has practically no breasts..." [117]) discovers that she has no sexual passion for Ronny, the man she is to marry; alternatively Aziz "a handsome little Oriental" (151) piques her curiosity. The occasion is ripe for disaster. V.A. Shahane, in accordance with various critical interpretations, sums up a 'minority critical view' that "Adela is sexually charmed by Aziz and that in her subconscious self she desires to be raped by him".[6] Thus it is that sexuality and repression enter the gap at the heart of the novel. The act of transgression, the rape, is a re-enactment of what Patricia Joplin has called the rivalries at work within the culture and the novel upon the body of a woman who, along with the experience is potentially silenced and elided.[7] Read in these terms the violation in the cave, far from being merely an implosion of sexual desire or repression, becomes a deployment of sexuality within a discourse of power that takes as its object both gender difference and racial difference. Cutting across biological and racial lines it constructs definitions of sexuality within a sex/gender/power system.

One of the uses that Forster puts fiction to is to explore and explode prevailing sexual attitudes and myths. In this context it can be safely said that *A Passage to India* is predominantly a novel about men and 'male homosocial desire'.[8] It relates their efforts to explore continents, cultures and races in order to understand and even to love one another. The source for the title of the novel is Walt Whitman's poem 'Passage to India':

Lo, soul, seest thou not God's purpose from the first?
The earth to be spann'd, connected by network,
The races, neighbours, to marry and be given in marriage,
The oceans to be cross'd, the distant brought near,
The lands to be welded together. (11. 31-35)

Referring exclusively jto men—to Christopher Columbus, Vasco da Gama, Aurangzeb, Tamerlane, Alexander the Great, Ibn Batouta—the poem details their adventures and exploits through the Old World and the New. The journey implicit in the title is a purely male endeavour. The 'marriage' alluded to is not the conjoining of male and female but of continents, of males, of masculine knowledge and discoveries.

That Forster shares Whitman's vision is made amply clear in the novel: "The world", says Fielding, "is a globe of men who are trying to reach one another and can best do so by the help of goodwill plus culture and intelligence" (62). To read Fielding as merely the alter ego of Forster may be pushing the issue but events in the novel repeatedly give credence to Fielding's assertion. At a certain point in the story Aziz and an Englishman develop a passing affection for each other while playing a game of polo. They part amicably and the narrator offers the following comment: "Nationality was returning, but before it could exert its poison, they parted saluting each other. 'If only they were all like that', each thought" (57).

Forster's novel, unlike Whitman's poem, is not totally blind to the female presence. The two central female characters, Mrs. Moore and Adela Quested are delineated in detail—both with their separate approaches to life as a whole and India in particular. But their main part is played out within the patriarchal and imperialist structures of the novel. Mrs. Moore initially promises to disrupt the prevailing pattern through her friendship with the young doctor. But her eventual descent into the character of a cranky and petulant old woman removes her from the scene of the interracial friendship and renders her meaningless. Obviously she is not capable of participating in the union of nations.

As for Adela, her significance lies in the role of facilitator; she provides the opportunity for Fielding and Aziz to meet. She exemplifies, in the words of Eve Kosofsky Sedgwick, "the use of women as exchangeable, perhaps symbolic, property for the primary purpose of cementing the bonds of men with men".[9] It is because of her desire to see the 'real India' that the two embark on their cross cultural friendship. When Fielding hosts a party for Mrs. Moore and Adela, Aziz is invited because of Adela's evident interest in him. Arriving early, Aziz strikes a rapport with Fielding and is disappointed when the two women turn up for, the narrator tells us, "he preferred to be alone with his new friend" (66). Adela's frightening experience in the caves helps to further cement the tie. It is largely at her expense that the relationship between the two men is tested and strengthened. A sceptical Fielding suggests a hallucinatory experience in the caves. Or, says he, the perpetrator of the sexual assault could have been the Indian guide who had entered the cave after her. In her last conversation with him Adela complacently adopts this suggestion. Once she retracts her account of the event in the caves Aziz's innocence is no longer in question. The incident at the Marabar Caves recedes into insignificance. It no longer matters to anyone what happened in the caves. Every belief in the text, ultimately even Adela's, seems to be part of a conspiracy to relegate the woman's experience to the peripheries of the story. The sexual assault is conveniently elided—one more testimony to the unreality, the 'muddledom' that is India.

Indian women fare little better in Forster's scheme of things. For the most part they are treated as nameless and invisible—Hamidullah's wife, Aziz's wife—with no claim to an existence apart from their husbands'. Left behind the purdah, Hamidullah's wife waits endlessly for her husband to show up and eat his dinner before she can eat hers; her incessant chatter is the only thing she has at her command. Aziz's dead wife is reduced to a medium, a means, for strengthening the bonds between the men. Aziz demonstrates his affection and esteem for Fielding by allowing the Englishman to see his dead wife's photograph. Fielding accepting this rare gesture of friendship with suitable gratitude is told that had Aziz's wife been alive Fielding would have been permitted to see her despite the purdah. "All men are my brothers and as soon as one behaves as such he may see my wife" (114), declares an emotionally charged Aziz. In Forster's vision when all men recognize their brotherhood there will no longer be any need for the seclusion of women. There is no place here for the wife's desire or will—indeed, like all other experiences involving women in the novel it is elided into silence. Within the mobile discursive field of what Foucault defines as relationships of power, subject and object may shift but the category of woman as object remains unchanging and forever fixed.[10]

Concerned primarily with valorizing the interracial dialogue between men Forster's treatment of womanhood becomes even more problematic when it is juxtaposed against the feminized image of India projected by the text. The British masculine gaze fixes India in the eternal

role of seductive, titillating and irresistible female object. Behind Adela
speaks the knowing voice of the male narrator:

> How can the mind take hold of such a country?
> Generations of invaders have tried, but they remain in
> exile. The important towns they build are only retreats,
> their quarrels the malaise of men who cannot find their
> way home. India knows of this trouble. She knows of
> the whole world's trouble, to its uttermost depth. She
> calls 'Come' through her hundred mouths, through
> objects ridiculous and august. But come to what? She
> has never defined. She is not a promise, only an appeal.
> (135)

Here is India, the colonized and feminized land mass, constructed in the
endlessly reiterated image of the East as tantalizing siren, all appeal and
no substance.

The rhetoric of power manifests itself in reductive strategies that
invalidate the other in ways that negate the irreducibility and multiplicity
of the human subject. In the course of the novel both the Indians and
the English indulge freely in a sardonic disparagement of the other race.
Ronny, the new City Magistrate is referred to as the "red nosed boy"
(13) because, for the Indians, the English apart from certain physical
differences are essentially indistinguishable: "They all become exactly
the same, not worse, not better. I give any Englishman two years, be
he Turton or Burton. It is only the difference of a letter. And I give any
Englishwoman six months" (13).

The English in their turn also generalize, unwilling to break free from
the representation of the category, 'Indian', painstakingly constructed
by the labour of generations of colonialists. The first mention made
about Aziz by the English successfully reduces the man—vital, alive and
interesting—to "some native subordinate or other" who had typically
failed to show up when needed; in the same breath Ronny is referred to as
"the type we want, he's one of us" (26). Caught up in a rhetoric of power
the English 'know' the Indians as 'types'. They little realise that within this
conceptual framework they themselves are reduced to a type—the White
Man—with a fixed set of gestures, opinions and attitudes. In *A Passage
to India* it is Ronny, the new Magistrate, who unequivocally enacts the
ideological power inherent in the racial discourse. In his zealous desire to
measure up to his compatriots' expectations he continually uses "phrases
and arguments that he had picked up from older officials" (54) to describe

the Indians, reducing them not only to an insulting physical state but also equating this with a general defective mental and moral character. Access to the rhetoric of power provides Ronny with the wherewithal to 'know' the Indians. After his inconsiderate disruption of the tea party at Fielding's, where he rudely ignores Aziz and Godbole, he insists he 'knows' Aziz to be the "spoilt Westernized type" (75). "No one who's here matters", he declares dismissively at the Bridge Party, "those who matter don't come" (39). In one stroke he reduces the Indians present from the status of objects to a state of invisibility and non-existence. A relentless logic marks the movement from Ronny's offensiveness to McBryde the policeman's theory of the depraved Indian male: effeminate, sexually promiscuous, attracted to the white English female.

In *A Passage to India* it is, therefore, difficult to discern any perspective but a Western one, or any gender but the masculine gender. The English and the Indians are locked in a power relationship and a discourse of race in which each treats the other as object. The only point at which the two intersect is in a discourse of sexuality where both maintain their position as subject, objectifying, silencing and eliding the woman. Even Fielding, liberal as he is in his attitude to the Indians, cannot hide his resentment at the disaster in the caves: "I knew these women would make trouble." Mrs. Moore clear sightedly knows this for what it is—an attempt at scapegoating women: "This man, having missed the train, tries to blame us" (156).

Forster himself cannot be said to have escaped the malaise. Elaine Showalter goes so far as to say that "we must accept the fact that Forster often saw women as part of the enemy camp".[11] In a 1922 article for *The Nation and the Athenaeum* he acerbically remarks:

> If the Englishman might have helped the Indian socially, how much more might the Englishwoman have helped! But she has done nothing, or worse than nothing.... She has instigated the follies of her male when she might have calmed them and set him on the sane course.[12]

For Forster the woman is infinitely more to blame for the appalling social situation in India; all the social and racial blunders are laid at her doors. It is the women who force men to choose sides. Fielding, Forster's alter ego, voices this early in the novel: "He had discovered that it is possible to keep in with Indians and Englishmen, but he who would also keep in with Englishwomen must drop the Indians. The two wouldn't combine" (62).

The real victim of the rape is actually perceived to be the man whose property—the woman—has been violated and defiled by a forcible usurpation of her body. Fielding, however, refuses to stand up for Ronny, the 'insulted fiancé', 'the martyr' (182). His resistance is to be read within a social system that is predicated on male bonding and male rivalry. In such a system the woman's experience, even of rape, is elided. In choosing Aziz over Ronny, Fielding affirms, at least potentially, a discourse of sexuality in which the shared gender mediates racial difference.[13] He attempts to retrieve Aziz from the elision which threatens to engulf him at his arrest and tries to restore his status as subject by reinstating him within the sexual discourse shared by men. Within this discourse Aziz and Fielding, both men, are both subjects, both in a position of power.

McBryde, the policeman, refusing to recognize Aziz as man, as subject, disrupts this honeymoon of shared sexuality. Once accused of rape Aziz is reduced to the status of an object. In discussing Aziz McBryde tells Fielding:

> You see, Fielding,....you're a schoolmaster, and consequently you come across these people at their best. That's what puts you wrong. They can be charming as boys. But I know them as they really are....
> (166)

In court, enunciating what he calls a "general truth" he states "a fact which any scientific observer will confirm" that "the darker races are physically attracted by the fairer, but not *vice versa*" (213).

When Aziz regains his freedom he reclaims the violated photograph of his wife appropriated and defiled by McBryde's possession; with it he regains his lost manhood. But the lost intimacy with Fielding is not restored. Fielding, or so Aziz believes, has broken the brotherhood bond by marrying Stella, his Anglo-Indian countrywoman. Fielding too, now married and committed to a system which defines him as English and male, is reluctant to continue the tenuous relationship with this colonized other. Moreover the feminized Indian landscape, with its hundred voices, prevents the reconciliating embrace: "No not yet.... No not there" (317). The gesture, says Edward Said, reinforces "a sense of the pathetic distances still separating 'us' from an Orient destined to bear its foreignness as mark of its permanent estrangement of the West."[14] And yet, the real "mark of permanent estrangement" that separates the two cultures is inscribed on the body of the woman who enters the caves and emerges speaking rape.

NOTES

1. G.K. Das, *E.M. Forster's India* (London: Macmillan, 1977), xiv.

2. Lionel Trilling, *E.M. Forster: A Study* (London: The Hogarth Press, 1944), 161.

3. Abdul R. JanMohamed, The Economy of Manichean Allegory'. *The Post Colonial Studies Reader*. Ed. Bill Ashcroft et al. (London: Routledge, 1995), 18-23.

4. E.M. Forster, *A Passage to India*, 1924 (Harmondsworth: Penguin, 1964), 203. Further references will appear in the text.

5. Letter to G.L. Dickinson, June 26, 1924; quoted in the Introduction to the Abinger edition of *A Passage to India* by E.M. Forster. Ed. Oliver Stallybrass (London: Edward Arnold, 1978), xxvi.

6. V.A. Shahane, *E.M. Forster. 'A Passage to India': A Study* (Delhi: OUP, 1977), 31.

7. Patricia K. Joplin, The Voice of the Shuttle is Ours', *Stanford Literary Review*, 1.1 (1984), 25-53.

8. See Eve Kosofsky Sedgwick, *Between Men* (New York: Columbia University Press, 1985).

9. Sedgwick, 25-26.

10. See Michel Foucault, *The History of Sexuality, Vol I: An Introduction* trans. Robert Hurley (1978; New York: Vintage, 1980).

11. Elaine Showalter, '*A Passage to India* as "Marriage Fiction": Forster's Sexual Politics', *Women & Literature* 5.2 (1977), 3-16.

12. E.M. Forster, 'Reflections in India: I—Too Late. *The Nation and the Athenaeum*, 30 Jan. 1922: 614-15.

13. Brenda R. Silver, 'Periphrasis, Power and Rape in *A Passage to India*'. *Post Colonial Theory and English Literature: A Reader*. Ed. Peter Childs (Edinburgh University Press, 1999), 370.

14. Edward Said, *Orientalism* (1978; New York: Vintage, 1979), 244.

5

The Soul's Voyage in Forster's *A Passage to India*
Alka Saxena

Since time immemorial man has been intrigued by the mystery of life and death. Scientific discoveries and developments have yet to unravel this mystery. Mankind is aware of the existence of that unseen power which pervades the whole universe. Spiritual quest lies beyond the purview of science and technology. Spiritualism is about the divine experience that can be felt through the process of self-realization. Mankind has yet to make a breakthrough in actually arriving at a conclusion about the exact nature and form of that Divine Spirit. Shelley's lines from *Adonais* also speak about the Absolute that can be experienced only after Death:

> The One remains, the many change and pass;/ Heaven's light forever shines, Earth's shadows fly/.... Until Death tramples it to fragments. Die,/ If thou wouldst be with that which thou dost seek! (Stanza 52)

Adonais is a deeply philosophical work. Shelley raises the question, "Whence are we, and why are we? Of what scene/ The actors or spectators?" (Stanza 21). The answer to this eternal question lies in the poem itself. According to Shelley, there is only one Universal Power or Spirit which pervades the entire Creation. It is omnipresent and it animates every particle of the universe. The poem presents a transcendental consolation for mortal loss and tries to assess man's place in this universe. The same mysticism is found in the works of Wordsworth. In the *Immortality Ode* he talks of the time when "meadow, grove and stream/ The earth, and every common sight/ To me did seem/ Apparelled in celestial light" (Stanza 1).

In *Tintern Abbey* he confesses that "The sounding cataract/ Haunted me like a passion: the tall rock,/ The mountain, and the deep and gloomy wood,/ Their colours and their forms, were then to me/ An appetite".

This stage finally led the poet to the spiritual love of Nature, a stage in which he realized the existence of a harmony between Nature and the immortal Soul. He now visualized "A motion and a spirit, that impels/ All thinking things, all objects of all thought/ And rolls through all things" (ll. 100-02).

The Romantic poets continue to fascinate the readers and writers alike because of the mystical element which marks their works. An art is an art whether expressed in the form of painting, music, poetry or fiction. The relationship between Nature and the soul of man that is seen in the poems discussed in the preceding paragraphs is also observed in Forster's *A Passage to India*.

In this novel, Mrs. Moore undergoes a psychic experience in the Marabar Caves. The echoes in the caves "Om-boum" that Mrs. Moore hears, are similar to the Hindu mantra of "Om". Although the vision in the caves is blurred (no ultimate description of the Divine Form exists) the results produced on her are similar to those produced at the moment of *Nirvana*, when the individual soul (*Atma*) merges with the Supreme Soul (*Parmatma*). The present paper examines Forster's masterpiece exclusively as a passage for the soul.

A Passage to India holds the interest of the readers even today. The reason for this interest can be attributed to that mystic element which runs throughout the novel. The novel operates at different levels for different people. For some it is a novel that deals primarily with the racial issues—the East-West confrontation; for others it is a study of human relationships or a study of the British Raj in India. Perhaps, at the superficial level it is all these but, at the core, it unravels the spiritual vision of life.

Forster's literary career spans the first quarter of the twentieth century which was marked by a loss of ethical and moral values as a result of the devastating War and destruction that followed. It was an age of disillusionment and decay. *A Passage to India* appeared two years later than T.S. Eliot's *The Wasteland*. Conditions in post-war England were disheartening. Post-war Europe was indeed a wasteland—a morally and spiritually barren land. It was a land of moral and spiritual decay and sterility. T.S. Eliot's *The Wasteland* is the most convincing presentation of the spiritual decay, frustration and disillusionment after the First World War. The 1920s was a decade in which the English people were recovering from the shock of World War I and hoping desperately that things would fall in place. They were looking for order in disorder. The War had inflicted physical as well as psychological wounds and the world was in utter chaos.

Forster responded to the problems that he saw around him. He was sensitive to the decline of spiritual values, the hatred that had crept into the people of different cultures and creed, the overall loss of faith, security and hope. Forster was not the lone sufferer. Many other poets and novelists also felt the decay of moral values in society. One cannot forget the eternal note of sadness in Matthew Arnold's *Dover Beach*. Arnold describes the contemporary world which had "neither joy, nor love, nor light/ Nor certitude, nor peace, nor help for pain." It was a darkling plain, "Swept with confused alarms of struggle and flight/ Where ignorant armies clash by night."

Writers of the early twentieth century were greatly perturbed by the spiritual vacuum and tried to find order by turning back to the Divine Spirit, be it the renewed faith in the Resurrection of Christ as viewed by Auden in *Musee Des Beaux Arts* or T.S. Eliot's faith in the possibility of purification and rejuvenation even in the contemporary spiritual wasteland. The possibility of a spiritual awakening or rebirth is a recurring theme in *The Wasteland*. In Part V Eliot offers a piece of advice to the modern hollow men telling them that they can regulate their lives through the principles of Datta, Dayadhvam and Damyata i.e. Charity, Compassion and Self-restraint. These principles lead to the process of self-realization through which man can experience oneness of the soul within himself. This concept can be achieved by adhering to the motto that Forster propagates i.e. 'Only Connect'. Following the convention of classical poems, *The Wasteland* too ends on a note of optimism.

Similarly, faced with the ugly realities of the materialistic world, Forster tried to give his own vision of life in his novels. It is an established fact that of all the genres of literature, the novel has mirrored honestly the complex life of modern age. E.M. Forster set out to modify the traditional novel by giving intellect a greater share in its creation and development. Later, in *Aspects of the Novel*, though he retained the story and the plot in his novels, he questioned the real need of these elements in the form of the novel. Following Meredith, he took the conception of the novel as a 'vehicle of philosophy' a stage further. In his novels the theme became more important than the plot and the characters. It is well known that Forster said, "Yes oh dear, yes—the novel tells a story...I wish that it was not so, that it could be something different—melody or perception of the truth, not this low atavistic form." Forster believed that there was more in a novel than time or people. He laid emphasis on the elements of fantasy and prophesy. Prophesy, he thinks implies the moral thesis or the mystical element that underlies and runs through all his works.

Two very characteristic themes of Forster are failure to connect and transcendental realities. In this respect *Howards End* and *A Passage to*

India leave a deep impact on the minds of his readers. The motto given in *Howards End* is 'Only Connect'. The main theme of the novel concerns the contrasting values of the Schlegels and Wilcoxes. It presents the conflict between the hardboiled materialistic sect represented by the Wilcoxes and the set of characters steeped in moral and aesthetic values denoted by the Schlegels. The Schlegels have a spiritual vision of life and through their vision the novelist aims to save the Wilcoxes. Reconciliation is possible only through the spiritual connection. The vision of the Wilcoxes was limited. It could be made infinite only through the enobling vision of the Schlegels, who possessed a sensitive understanding of moral and aesthetic values. Margaret Schlegel stands for the 'inner life of the soul'. Thus, Margaret's marriage with the Senior Wilcox is symbolic. By this connection, through marriage the soul of Mr. Wilcox is to be saved. A truly balanced life is possible when Wilcox and Schlegel unite. This union will also be gainful to Margaret who will get "Howards End", the house which symbolizes the heart of England and which mystically holds the secret of true personal understanding. The novel lays emphasis on the connection of two modes of life. It is a remarkable attempt at the theme of reconciliation.

Looking beyond the two classes represented by the Wilcoxes and the Schlegels, Forster seems to draw our attention to the fact that amidst chaos man can find order only through mysticism. A critical assessment the work of *A Passage to India* clearly indicates this belief. After several readings, *A Passage to India* stands out as a purely philosophical novel. L.P. Hartley saw the book as intensely personal and intensely cosmic. That Forster meant it to be a philosophic treatise can be established by reading the opening and closing sentences of this remarkable work.

The closing sentence apparently seems to offer the possibility of a reconciliation of the East and the West. But seen from a different perspective it makes one understand that "the earth didn't want it" and the sky said "No, Not there" is just the beginning of the statement which has to be connected with the opening lines "except for the Marabar Caves" (31) which are "extraordinary" (31). In my observation, the complete sentence seems to answer man's quest for spiritualism in the following manner, "The answer does not lie in the vast purview between the sky and the earth, but deep down in the extraordinary realms of the Marabar Caves."

In the first few paragraphs of the novel the adjective 'extraordinary' is used twice to describe the Marabar Caves. Forster writes, "These fists and fingers are the Marabar hills containing the extraordinary caves" (31). The repetition of this very potent word lays emphasis on the fact that the Marabar Caves are mysterious yet fascinating because in them lies the real meaning of life. Man's quest for the self, the process of self-realization is actually an inward journey. In order to understand the mystery of life one has to retrace his steps. Instead of going out, reaching for the sky, or searching around on earth, he has to turn back and look deep within himself. There is a difference between Religion and Spiritualism. Religion can imply the reading of scriptures and following of rituals and ceremonies. A religious man lives in the narrow divisions of caste, race and gender. But spiritualism is infinite. It has no watertight compartments or sections and therefore, Forster observes that a spiritual quest cannot be undertaken within the limited vision of man, which incidentally stretches vastly between the earth and the sky. But this vastness is not expansive, it is a linear vision. A true seeker of the Ultimate invariably seeks within himself. He retreats to the inner silence in the deep caves, the inner recesses of the heart and mind. The ability to travel within and to ultimately unite with the higher consciousness is 'extraordinary' and it is towards the attainment of this 'extraordinary' goal that man must strive in order to achieve inner peace, total bliss— *Nirvana*.

Mrs. Moore's visit to the Marabar Caves suddenly accentuates her spiritual progress. The title, *A Passage to India*, means not only an actual passage on a ship but also a passage of the soul and this is symbolized in the visit to the caves and in the nightmare experience of the echo which Mrs. Moore has in them. She is presented as a religious woman right from the beginning. It would be worthwhile to study her spiritual progress in order to understand the mystic element in the novel. In Chapter 5 she talks to Ronny about the bad and un-Christian treatment of the British towards the Indians. She believes that since God loves everyone and India is part of the earth God loves Indians too. Her belief that God is love corresponds with the similar concept of *Satyam, Shivam, Sundaram* which is prevalent in Indian philosophy.

Both Mrs. Moore and Adela are genuinely interested in knowing the real India. They are eager to have the real Indian experience in the country. In contrast, Aziz, despite being an Indian, is more loyal to his religion. Aziz feels renewed and at home in the Mosque. His body and spirit are united by his religion in the Mosque. He seems to be more loyal to Islam than to his country. In Chapter 14 he tells Mrs. Moore that he cannot accept the Hindu notion of universality. He feels it is best if everyone adheres to his own religion.

Mrs. Moore's spiritual quest follows the pattern of inquiry, frustration, dilemma and integration, culminating in the final revelation. The journey to the caves symbolizes the concept of Nothingness and Emptiness which is a very integral concept of Indian mysticism. The caves are hollow and vacant and suggest that man's limited consciousness simply cannot face this enormous expanse of time.

In the extraordinary caves, Forster perceived all the mystery he sensed in India. In the section entitled *The Caves*, the key incident of the novel unfolds dramatically. In the last three paragraphs of Chapter XII the caves take on a mysterious quality. The focus is at first on the physical details of the caves and on the visitors' experiences and feelings about them. Then the mysterious capacity of the caves to reflect light is brought in. Forster approaches mystery through a seeming commonplace which is extraordinary. The caves appear to be so similar that it is impossible to distinguish one from the other. They are presented as mundane and "Nothing, nothing attaches to them" (138). The echo too is 'empty'. Darkness and emptiness make the caves monotonous and mysterious at the same time. The nothingness and emptiness cannot be ignored. On the contrary this arouses interest and curiosity. Forster stresses their emptiness and makes them appear potent only because they are meaningless and empty. The caves are important because they make the characters conscious of themselves. People question themselves when surrounded by the emptiness of the caves, thereby suggesting that their 'nothing' is in fact 'all'. Forster juxtaposes the mundane and the mystical.

In Chapter 14 when Mrs. Moore enters one of the caves, she has an experience of that Oneness which is Nothingness. This total negation destroys in a moment her entire system of values and beliefs. The Boum sound erases all religious thoughts from Mrs. Moore's mind. The echo becomes more powerful than her religion. She looses interest in religion and other aspects of life. For Mrs. Moore all and nothing become one.

The echo passes from Mrs. Moore to others as well. Mrs. Moore has been called a guardian in this sense. Her name is mispronounced as Esmiss, Esmoor and in this way unknowingly they have called her by the name of a Hindu goddess. This 'mistake' once again confirms her position as a guardian; she represents the mother figure—the female goddess. In Chapter twenty-four we see her effect on Adela, who now stays away from intellectual ways and begins praying again. Mrs. Moore appears in Godbole's head during a spell of spiritual fervor. The visit by Mrs. Moore completes him and brings him closer to God. Once again Forster reaffirms the faith that God is love. Thus, we find that Mrs. Wilcox and Mrs. Moore have a mystical link with the past and are able to connect with people from beyond their circle.

Forster's Indian connection is another aspect that needs to be established in order to understand the themes of his novels. Forster visited India in 1912-13 and 1921. Forster's two visits to India provided him much of the colour and feelings of the places which his novel reveals. He began writing the novel in 1913 but the First World War intervened and it did not get published till 1924. In the Editorial note to the novel,

Oliver Stallybrass writes "Forster's Passage to India had begun more than seventeen years before his 'A Passage to India' was published" (7). Stallybrass writes about Forster's association with Sir Syed Ross Masood, whom he taught Latin and whose association proved very fruitful. In his obituary to Masood, Forster writes "My own debt to him is incalculable. He woke me up...showed me new horizons and a new civilization, and helped me towards the understanding of a continent. Until I met him, India was a vague jumble of rajas, sahibs, babus and elephants.... He made everything real and exciting as soon as he began to talk, and seventeen years later when I wrote *A Passage to India*, I dedicated it to him..." (8). Through Masood, Forster got 'connected' to India and to other Indians, the most prominent being the Hindu Raja of Chattarpur. When Forster first came to India in 1912, he had already prepared himself by a wide course of reading some topical books on India. Like his characters, he too, perhaps wanted to know the real India and so he went further and also read religious and literary classics like the *Mahabharata* and Kalidasa's epic *Shakuntala*. He prepared himself on all fronts, for he had also inspected copies of the Ajanta cave frescoes and even made an acquaintance at the London Zoo, of some of the Indian animals, whose presence is marked throughout *A Passage to India*. In India he travelled and visited a lot of places as the guest of the Maharaja of Chattarpur. The region of Bandipore and Barabar Caves became the famous Chandrapore and Marabar caves in his novel.

Forster enjoyed the company of Indians. He preferred staying with Indians rather than being with the British at some club or other social gathering. On returning to England he translated his impressions, which took the form of *A Passage to India*. Before writing the novel he was clear about the chief characters and the racial tension that would be portrayed in it. He had also foreseen that something crucial would happen at the Marabar Caves.

Forster himself has confirmed that 'the book is not really about politics. It's about something wider than politics, about the search of the human race for a more lasting home, about the universe as embodied in the Indian earth and the Indian sky. He has stated that he desires it to be philosophic and poetic.

The motto 'only connect', again, seems to explain the significance of *A Passage to India*. The novel seems to suggest that in order to comprehend the real India one has to connect with the Indian ethos and mysticism. Forster's Programme Note to Santha Rama Rau's dramatized version of his novel reads as follows: "I tried to indicate the human predicament in a universe which is not so far, comprehensible to our minds" (336). Thus, we see that Forster's masterpiece was a fusion of realism and symbolism, of the personal and the cosmic. In *A Passage to India*, Forster's intention clearly is to present the East-West encounter, but more importantly, he wishes to communicate a much greater philosophy—a mystical, highly symbolic view of life, death and what lies beyond it. Lines from Walt Whitman's poem, *Passage to India*, which Forster took as the title for his novel sum up beautifully the entire thesis of the novel:

Passage to more than India

Are thy wings plumed indeed for such flights;

O Soul; voyagest thou indeed on voyages like those.

WORK CITED

Forster, E.M. *A Passage to India*. England: Penguin Books, 1982.

6

Cultural Misunderstandings in *A Passage to India*
Neeta Shukla

E.M. Forster, the English author and critic, a member of the Bloomsbury group and a friend of Virginia Woolf wrote five novels of which four appeared before World War I. Forster's major concern in his novels was that individuals should 'connect prose with passion' within themselves. Therefore, he says—"If human nature does alter it will be because individuals manage to look at themselves in a new way. Here and there people—a very few people, but a few novelists are among them—are trying to do this. Every institution and vested interest is against such a search: organized religion, the state, the family in its economic aspect. Have nothing to gain, and it is only when outward prohibitions weaken it can proceed; history conditions it to that extent" (*Aspects of the Novel*, 1927).

Between the years 1912 and 1913 Forster travelled in India and then in 1924 he again returned to India, working as a private secretary to the Maharaja of Dewas. The land became the scene of his masterpiece, *A Passage to India*, an account of India under the British rule. The novel is the story of Adela Quested, who visits Chandrapore under the chaperonage of Mrs. Moore in order to make up her mind regarding her marriage to the latter's son. Mrs. Moore and Adela are keen to explore India. Mrs. Moore's son Ronny does not appreciate their interest in wanting to know India and his mother and Adela cannot understand Ronny's attitude of the ruling class. Ronny stops his mother and Adela from making acquaintance outside the British community yet Mrs. Moore ventures into a mosque and meets Dr. Aziz who is at that moment hurt and miserable because of the behaviour of a British official. Mrs. Moore's interest in his problems and her extending a hand of friendship towards the latter placate him. Aziz and Mrs. Moore become friends and so does Adela later. They think that by knowing Indians they will know

India and Aziz too is happy at having made acquaintance with them. To please them he organizes a visit to the Marabar Caves. The party includes Mr. Fielding, the principal of a local college, Professor Godbole, a Hindu teacher and the two ladies. But these two men miss the train and Aziz travels ahead with the two ladies and his many helpers.

In one of the caves Mrs. Moore has a disturbing experience and she refrains from going any further. Adela while on the way ventures to discuss of love with Aziz the concept of love in general terms but this talk displeases and upsets him. In the cave she for a moment loses her sense of proportion and imagines that Aziz has attempted to rape her when her field glasses are accidentally pulled and broken by someone. The English, intolerant of Indians, treat this incident as outrageous and react hysterically. They readily believe in the accusation made by Adela and take Aziz to be guilty even before a verdict is passed. His lone supporters are Mr. Fielding and Mrs. Moore. Fielding likes this young doctor and Mrs. Moore is convinced about Aziz's innocence because of an intuition that Adela is gripped with illusions. Fielding who supports him is excluded from the proceedings and Mrs. Moore is sent back to England by her son. The journey sees her dead on the way as she could not bear the heat of an Indian summer. At the trial Adela gathers her nerves and her illusions get dispelled. She withdraws the charges levelled against Aziz who is thus exonerated and released from lock-up. Fielding's faith in Aziz is accepted and he is promoted. The Indians are happy with the justice meted out to them at the expense of the English.

The novel without prejudice draws the dissimilarities among the British, Hindus and Muslims. The English believe in their superiority and so they care little for the emotions of the Indians and in turn their behaviour reflects their arrogance, insensitivity and rudeness. The women are shown to be the most condescending in their attitude. Turton in the novel thinks, "after all it's our women who make everything more difficult out here". Indians on the other hand know that they are not appreciated by the English. Fielding says "Indians know whether they are liked or not...they cannot be fooled here. Justice never satisfies them, and that is why the British Empire rests on sand." Forster reflects a sympathetic leaning towards the Indians and shows how they are ruled by emotions rather than by independent thinking as a consequence of which their behaviour lacks maturity.

Mrs. Moore, who demonstrates independent thinking, does not take nicely to the comments made by Ronny about Indians and his defence of the British attitude towards them. "His words without his voice might have impressed her, but when she heard the self-satisfied lilt of them, when she saw the mouth moving so complacently and competently beneath the little red nose, she felt quite illogically, that this was not the last word on India." Ronny is clear about his views on the union of India and England and thinks about it as a political relationship. He tells his mother that the English were not in India to be pleasant but "to hold this wretched country by force". The English and Indians differ on this. Aziz in his illness tells Fielding that what India needs is "kindness, more kindness, and even after that more kindness. I assure you it is the only hope...we can't build up India except on what we feel." Even attempts made by either party are not enough to bring down the differences of the Indian Muslims, Indian Hindus and the English. Many things come between their relationship and mere liking and goodwill for each other are not enough.

Forster maintains objectivity in the novel and the perceptions he registers allow one to see that the principal concern in the novel is cultural misunderstanding. Differing cultural views and expectations regarding hospitality, social propriety and the role of religion in daily life are responsible for misunderstandings between the English and the Muslims, the English and the Hindus and between the Muslims and the Hindus. Aziz tells Fielding at the end of the novel "...It is useless discussing Hindus with me. Living with them teaches me no more. When I think I annoy them, I do not, when I think I don't annoy them, I do. Perhaps they will sack me for fumbling onto their doll's house; on the other hand perhaps they will double my salary. Time will prove..." (285). Aziz loves working in the hospital as his profession fascinates him at times but 'the boredom of regime and hygiene repelled him, and after inoculating a man for enteric he would go away and drink unfiltered water himself'. Major Callendar makes the remark "what could you expect from that fellow?" "No grit, no guts." But in his heart he knew that if Aziz not he had operated last year on Mrs. Grayford's appendix, the old lady would have probably lived. He does not divulge this and despite being an inferior surgeon maintains his superiority over the Indians.

The novel explores the most obvious gap between the Indians and the English. Chandrapore is divided as the native town and the English civil station from which the town "appears to be a totally different place" (8). The separation is complete, the civil station "shares nothing with the city except the overarching sky" (8). The bridge party is meant to bridge the gulf between the English and the Indians but ironically enough it only serves to emphasize it. The comments of Mrs. Turton on the Indian guests at the bridge party show that the attitude of the English ladies is one of supercilious disregard "Why they come at all I don't know. They hate it as much as I do. Talk to Mrs. Mcbryde. Her husband made her give purdah parties until she struck." She tells Mrs. Moore "You're superior to them anyway. Don't forget that. You're superior to everyone in India except one or two of the Rani's, and they're on equality" (33).

The cultural difference between Adela and Aziz are obvious in the conversation they have in the Marabar Caves. For Adela it is normal to discuss about love and marriage with anybody. For Aziz it is an act of sacrilege. As Adela goes with Aziz alone to explore a cave she asks Aziz "Are you married, Dr. Aziz?"

"Yes, indeed, do come and see my wife"—

"And have you any children?"

"Yes, indeed, three," he replied in firmer tones.

"Have you one wife or more than one?" she asks in her honest, decent, inquisitive way.

"The question shocked the young man very much. It challenged a new conviction of his community, and new convictions are more sensitive than old. If she had said, 'Do you worship one God or several?' he would not have objected. But to ask an educated Indian Muslim how many wives he has— appalling, hideous!" (135-36).

Aziz and Fielding reach out to each other in friendship but their respective cultures keep them apart. They do not understand each other's emotions. "Your emotions never seem in proportion to their objects, Aziz" Fielding says and Aziz answers "Is emotion a sack of potatoes... to be measured out?" Hindus and Muslims too fail to connect. Forster says in the novel, "Between people of distant climes there is always the possibility of a romance, but the various branches of Indians know too much about each other to surmount the unknowable easily." Aziz speaking in all friendliness to Mr. Das wishes that Hindus did not remind him of cow-dung and Mr. Das thinks "Some Moslems are very violent." The possibility of having a relationship between them is very remote as both are culturally miles apart.

Forster shows how these repeated misunderstandings become hardened into cultural stereotypes and are often used to justify the uselessness of attempts to bridge the cultural gulfs. When Aziz offers his collar stud to Fielding in an effusive act of friendship, Heaslop later misinterprets Aziz's missing stud as an oversight and extends it as a general example "...there you have the Indian all over, inattention to detail, the fundamental slackness that reveals the race" (69). On the incident of the carriage not reaching the ladies on time Aziz strikes out at Hindus. He says: "slack Hindus—they have no idea of society; I know them very well because of a doctor at the hospital. Such a slack unpunctual fellow. It is as well you did not go to their house, for it would give you a wrong idea of India. Nothing sanitary...."

Professor Godbole is never political. He never makes any remarks on the Muslims or the English and has been shown as a man of spirit alone—encompassing all in his love for Lord Krishna. Fielding asks him "Is Aziz innocent or guilty?" Godbole gives no personal opinion and feels the matter can best be resolved at the court. Yet though Fielding insists on a personal opinion to which Godbole links his views to his philosophy and generalizes good and evil as part of human action. Fielding fails to understand his reply and receives it in gloomy silence.

The Collector who had twenty-five years of experience in the country opines "...and during those twenty-five years I have never known anything but disastrons results when English people and Indians attempt to be intimate socially. Intercourse yes, courtesy, by all means. Intimacy never, never. Fielding and Mrs. Moore who want to defend Aziz cannot override the prejudices of the British against the Indians. Aziz retreats from Chandrapore to Mau, from the English and their Western science to a remote place where he can let his instruments rust, (run) his little hospital at half steam, and (cause) no undue alarm." He fails to overcome the cultural separations and gaps which divide him from the English. Even though Aziz forgives Adela in the name of Mrs. Moore and withdraws his suit of damages against her, she does not appeal to Hamidullah—

> If she had shown emotion in court, broken down... beat her and invoked the name of God, she would have summoned his imagination and generosity—he had plenty of both. But while relieving the Oriental mind she had chilled it, with the result that he could scarcely believe she was sincere, and indeed from his standpoint she was not. For her behaviour rested on cold justice and honesty; she had felt, while she recanted, no passion of love for those whom she had wronged. Truth is not truth in that exacting land unless there goes with it kindness and more kindness and kindness again, unless the word that was God also is God. And the girl's sacrifice—so creditable according to Western notions—was rightly rejected, because, though it came from her heart, it did not include her heart. A few garlands from students was all that India ever gave her in return.

Aziz, though is an Indian, at many times, fails to plumb the depth where the pristine culture and philosophy of India is concerned. The mystery of the Marabar could only be understood by a Hindu:

...he (Aziz) had no notion how to treat this particular aspect of India; he was lost in it without Professor Godbole like themselves.

At Mau the festival of Gokul Asthami, the united celebration by Hindus, is "not understood by Aziz anymore than any average Christian". Fielding admits to Aziz that he "never really understood or liked them (Hindus) except an occasional scrap of Godbole". Thinking of the cleavage in India Forster remarks "the fissures in the Indian soil are infinite: Hinduism, so solid from a distance, is riven into sects and clans, which radiate and join, and changes their names according to the aspect from which they are approached. Study it for years with the best teachers, and when you raise your head nothing they have told you quite fits."

The Indians are together only by virtue of antagonism towards and suspicion of the English. The Muslims and the Hindus, though separate groups, are united by their traditions, their history, their religion and their art. The novel explores the various aspects of the gulf between the English and the Indians and that between groups of Indians among themselves. All incidents show that cultural differences are deeply embedded and any attempt at intimacy fails. At the end of the novel this question is raised and Forster again seems to say that this is not possible—

> "Why cant we be friends now?" said (Fielding) holding him (Aziz) affectionately. "It is what you want. It's what you want."

But the horses didn't want it—they swerved apart; the earth didn't want it, sending up rocks through which riders must pass single file; the temples, the tank, the jail, the palace, the birds, the carrion, the Guest House that came into view as they issued from the gap and saw Mau beneath; they didn't want it, they said in their hundred voices, "No, not yet", and the sky said, "No, not there".

REFERENCES

Bradbury, Malcolm, ed. *E.M. Forster: A Passage to India* (London: Macmillan, 1979).

Forster, E.M. *A Passage to India* (New Delhi: Penguin Books, 1979).

—— *Aspects of the Novel* (Harmondsworth: Penguin, 1962).

Trilling, Lionel. *E.M. Forster: A Study* (London: Hogarth Press, 1944).

7

Thesis, Anti-thesis and Synthesis in Forster's *A Passage to India*
Nivedita Tandon

A Passage to India, E.M. Forster's last novel, was published in 1924. It became instantly famous as a novel which treated perceptively and looked sympathetically at the problem of "Anglo-India". A lot of critical work has been done to analyze *A Passage to India* as a social document: a book which no student of the Indian question can disregard (Peter Burra). Great emphasis has been laid on the element of mystery in the novel and plenty of work has been done on its plot, style, character, ideas and attitudes. An aspect which needs a lot of looking into is the theme of the novel keeping in mind the framework of thought in it which has often led to a misunderstanding among critics, so much so that critics have made statements like "one can re-read (the novel) a dozen times and be no nearer to the solution".[1]

Any serious reader of Forster is able to discern that his novels are replete with suggestions and indeed it is a difficult task to translate suggestive and poetic language into explicit statement without destroying some reality. However, this task would not be so difficult if a reader were to concentrate on the way Forster has given life and force to the thought pattern which accounts for the basic theme of the novel.

The dominant idea of *A Passage to India* is best expressed in the following poem of Walt Whitman's poem from where the title has been taken:

A Passage to India,
To soul, sees't thou not God's purpose from the first?
The earth to be spanned, connected by network,
The races, neighbours, to marry and to be given in marriage,
The ocean to be crossed, the distant brought near,
The lands to be wedded together.[2]

It is the theme of fission and fusion, of separateness and of desired union that governs the novel. The threefold division of the book into 'Mosque', 'Caves' and 'Temple' which Forster himself tells us represents the divisions of the Indian year, the Cold Weather, the Hot Weather and the Rains. It also represents Thesis—Anti thesis—Synthesis or the statement of the problem and two opposite solutions—a dialectical pattern.

In Part I, 'Mosque', the central problem of division seems to manifest itself everywhere. The gap between the Indians and the English is represented by Chandrapore—the town divided into the native section and the "English Civil Station from which the town appears to be a totally different place" (3).[3] The separation is complete, "the civil station shares nothing with the city except the overarching sky" (3). This is the first hint of separation; the very surroundings seem to hint the division which seems to be more fundamental than any human difference.

Similarly India is not one but a hundred entities among which the Hindus and Moslems are the most noticeable. India is a land of diversity a seeming muddle which cannot be summed up by any single race, creed, caste or person.

It is, however, difficult to distinguish the diversity: "nothing in India is identifiable, the mere asking of a question causes it to disappear or to merge into something else" (81). India is presented throughout as the very place of division, the happy continent where separation is felt more profoundly than in other places; and later, we learn that Aziz's picnic fails "because he had challenged the spirit of the Indian earth, which tries to keep men in compartments" (122).

The division is not only in the continent and its inhabitants; its conquerors are equally disunited. The English, in their club from which all Indians are excluded, are divided among themselves by the same barriers. Those who have been for some time in India are different in outlook from the newcomers, who have not yet retreated behind the defenses of tradition, race, caste and position. Major officials look down upon the minor officials; likewise the wives look down upon their inferior sisters. Among the British there is a separation among the sexes, almost an antagonism; the women think their men 'weak' in dealing with the natives; the men believe that it is their women who complicate matters.

Though there is a lot of disunity, division and separation that is rampant yet there is also a desire for some sort of unity. Separated from each other by race, caste, religion, sex, age, occupation and other such barriers of life men must still make an effort to unite with each other and to achieve some harmonious resolution of their differences 'Mosque' is not only a symphony of differences but of attempts at oneness. But this unity which is sought is of two different kinds, which must be carefully distinguished. "One is the unity of negation, the other of affirmation, of exclusion, the other of inclusion. The other reconciles them in a larger synthesis. The one merely breeds misunderstanding, violence and hatred, the other seeks peaceful resolution."[4]

The first kind of unity is easy to understand. The common binding factor among the Indians is the mutual suspicion and hatred against the English. Hatred and suspicion of the British is a force strong enough to unite different races and creeds. The Muslims and the Hindus are united by common history, tradition, religion and art. For Aziz and his friends, quoting the poetry of Islam, India is one and their own. Aziz, visiting his mosque, finds the home of his spirit in that faith. But at the same time it is this very unity which sets the various elements apart. Aziz, embracing a Hindu friend, thinks, 'I wish they did not remind me of cow dung' at the same time his friend is thinking; 'some Moslems are violent' (262). The British also encounter the unity of exclusion, of suspicion and of hatred. The anthem of the army of occupation reminds each one of them about their 'exile' and for some time enables them to sink their differences and prejudices within themselves. "Unity of this kind is achieved not 'with' but 'against', it is essentially hostile and evil in nature, and the breeder of more hostility and more evil."[5]

The first kind of unity affirms the differences and separation natural to life, the second attempts to embrace and to reconcile them by goodwill, sympathy, kindness and love. The effort may be on either a purely secular level, or on a religious basis. Fielding, the 'holy man minus the holiness' (116), believes that the world is a globe of men who are trying to reach one another and can best do so by the help of goodwill plus culture and intelligence' (57). Adela desires to 'see the real India' (19), to learn and to understand. She is endowed with true goodwill but she is deficient in emotional response, in the 'secret understanding of the heart' (15). From this deficiency stem all her future problems.

In the 'Mosque' the gulf between the English and Indians is shown from both points of view, at the dinner in Hamidullah's home and in the English club, at the farcical 'Bridge Party'. However, when Aziz, the Indian, meets the newcomers who wish to communicate, to bridge the gap between them by offering genuine goodwill, kindness, even love, instantly he responds to Mrs. Moore's efforts at understanding him at their meeting in the mosque, instantly he makes friends with Fielding. Though he does not really like Adela, he generously makes plans for the ladies visit to the Marabar Caves. At the end of this section it seems that brotherhood is about to Triumph. East and West have met and embraced; friendship and love are in the ascendant. The Mosque, a symbol of Islam preaches the oneness of God. Christianity, the religion of the English, teaches the concept of the oneness of all men in Divine Love. The season of the year is the cold weather, most suitable to human life and activity; the climate in which men can grow and live. But 'April, herald of horrors' (110) is close at hand, the Hot Weather, dangerous and oppressive to all life. Prof. Godbole, the Hindu, has has invoked his Lord Krishna "Come, Come, Come..." (75). But the God refuses to come.

   " 'Mosque' is the thesis, the problem of separation and attempts at bridging the gulf, 'Caves' is the Antithesis, for in it we see the rout of the forces of reconciliation, the triumph of evil, hostility and negation."[6]

The central action of this part and of the entire novel is the experience of the two English women, Adela Quested and Mrs. Moore in the Marabar Caves. It is a shattering experience, disastrous to everyone: it destroys Mrs. Moore both spiritually and physically; 'it drives Adela to the brink of madness; it threatens to bring ruin to Aziz, and actually alters his entire future; it imperils all relations between the English and the Indians; and it destroys all constructive relationships between individuals. Yet it is never satisfactorily explained by the author. The nature and meaning of Adela's and Mrs. Moore's experiences are left in darkness, dealt with only in highly oblique and allusive language.

The Marabar Caves are the very voice of that union which is the opposite of divine, the voice of evil and negation, of that universe which is "older than all spirit" (119). The answer they give to the problem of oneness is an answer of despair and horror, whether on the human or on the universal level.

To each woman the voice of the Marabar Caves speaks of a kind of oneness, but in different terms, terms appropriate to character, age and situation. To Mrs. Moore the echo "speaks of a universe in which all differences have been annihilated, Infinity of Nothing. Good and evil are identical. Everything exists, nothing has value" (144). All has become one; but the one is Nothing. To Adela, who has wished to understand but not love India and the Indians, who has become engaged to a man she does not love, who is not convinced that love is necessary to a successful union, the meaning of the echo presents itself in different tensions. To her, it speaks of the last horror of union by force and fear, without love she believes that Aziz has attemped to assault her, goes nearly mad with horror and sets in motion the machinery that shall prosecute and punish him. For the Marabar Caves have revealed to her what such a union is: Rape. Upon Mrs. Moore has dawned the futility of a union between Indians and the English, she is disillusioned. She felt increasingly that "...though people are important the relations between them are not, and that in particular too much fuss has been made over marriage, centuries of carnal embracement, yet man is no nearer to understanding man. And today she felt with such force that it seemed itself a relationship, itself a person, who was trying to take hold of her hand" (130). In this state of mind she enters the Marabar Caves and hears the echo of that oneness which is nothingness. She loses interest in everything from this moment. She dismisses Adela's experience as rubbish. Though she knows of Aziz's innocence she neither speaks nor stays to testify at his trial. She leaves in this season of Hot weather when travel is dangerous and dies at sea. The echo has ended everything for her. To the Christian Mystic the Marabar has said that the universe is a muddle rather than a mystery; the answer to its riddle is nothingness.

To Adela the meaning of the echoes is different but equally disastrous. She has nurtured an arid intellectualism. Her goodwill, her kindness do not come from the heart, they come from the head. Fielding points out that she has failed because she has no real affection for Aziz or the Indians. Adela's engagement happens to reflect the same forces that unite the English against the outsiders. She is marrying Ronny, not out of love. She had earlier refused to marry him, but because of the accident of the Nawab Bahadur's car she is now engaged to him. When she enters the Caves for the first time she realizes that she and Ronny do not love each other. The analogy here between the personal situation of Adela and Ronny and the political situation between Indian and England is clear. It is almost a forced union. As Adela feels about her union with Ronny so does Ronny feel about the union of India and England politically. He tells his mother that the English were not in India to be pleasant but to 'hold this wretched country by force' (45). The English were holding India by fear and force, without kindness or love. 'Mosque' is full of this sort of union: hostile, negative and evil. Now Adela, joined to Ronny without love, by the same forces which operate to link together the English in India against the native and outsider, experiences symbolically the utmost degradation of such a union.

"The effect of their experience in the Marabar is to quench every little flame of kindness and goodwill in those around them. The bridges thrown across the gulfs crumble; the abysses widen and deepen. Evil and negative unity alone is left. As a result the English draw together more firmly than ever against natives in a union that destroys all justice and mercy. Fear and hate unite the Indians in Aziz's defence. The evil spreads and propagates itself the spirit of violence stalks abroad; the echo of the Marabar, spouting from its cave has spread until it threatens to engulf the lives of everyone. Though Mrs. Moore has averted the ultimate disaster, nothing good is left. Marabar has brought nothing but evil. Political relationships have been endangered, personal ones fare no better. Adela is rejected by the English community, Ronny breaks his engagement. Fielding, cast out by his fellowmen, is misunderstood by the Indians, his friendship with Aziz wrecked by the latter's suspicion of treachery. Kindness and goodness have failed; of all the hopes and tentative gestures of union in Part I nothing is left but hatred, force and fear. The Marabar has triumphed."[7]

'Temple', the title of the third section of the novel, is the symbol of the Hindu religion, of a possible reconciliation of differences not in negation but in a larger synthesis, of a universe which is perhaps a mystery rather than a muddle, a riddle to which an answer exists; and of the Rains, token of renewed life, of regeneration, and of hope.

'Temple' seems to bring about reconciliation after the horrible breakdown, conflict and the charm created between the English and the Indians in the 'Loves'. This reconciliation is wrought through Professor Godbole, a Hindu mystic, totally immersed in the life of the spirit, philosophical and utterly impractical. He seems to personify the Hindu creed which stands for universality. Hinduism talks about synthesis— all creation is part of each other and all are part of the divine. The evil and good alike express the whole of the universe, further, good and evil are both aspects of God. He is present in one and absent in the other. Godbole stands, in reality, for the union of all men, whether they will or no, and for a universe in which God exists, though he may at a particular time and place not be present for a universe which may be a mystery but is not a muddle.

'Universality' is the theme of the festival of Lord Krishna with which the section, 'Temple', opens. At the birth of the God "all sorrow was annihilated, not only for Indians, but for foreigners, birds, caves, railways, and the stars, all became joy, all laughter; there had never been disease nor doubt, misunderstanding, cruelty, fear (283). The voice of Marabar is drowned in this festival, in which 'Infinite Love took upon itself the form of Sri Krishna, and saved the world" (282). In 'Temple' the effects of the Marabar Caves are cancelled and reconciliation takes places on the human level. Reconciliation, not real union, Painful human differences are soothed, Aziz and Fielding resume their friendship, though it can lead no further; Aziz finally makes his peace with Adela. These things are brought about by Mrs. Moore, who returns to India in the guise of her children, Stella, whom Fielding married, and Ralph, son of her spirit. Her memory, and the presence of her son, Ralph, completely change Aziz's attitude from hostility to homage. The Marabar has been wiped out. Synthesis takes place in the form of reconciliation.

"All invitations must proceed from heaven perhaps; perhaps it is futile for men to initiate their own unity, they do but widen the gulfs between them by the attempt" (32). So Forster seems to be saying. *A Passage to India* is a novel of these gulfs of the bridges thrown across them, of the tensions that hamper and threaten communication of the failure and the horror of all efforts at union without Love of whether Oneness when found is Something or Nothing. *A Passage to India* is the last and best of Forster's apparently final efforts to incarnate his difficult ideas; it is an attempt to fuse the real world of social comedy and human conflict with the meaning and value of the universe which that world mirrors.

NOTES

1. E.B.C. Jones, "E.M. Forster and Virginia Woolf", *The English Novelists* (ed.) Derek Verschoyle (1936), 262.

2. *Leaves of Grass*, Ind. ed. (New York, 1924), 343-51.

3. E.M. Forster, *A Passage to India* (London: Penguin, 1979). All references in the preceding article are from this edition.

4. Gertrude M. White, "'A Passage to India': Analysis and Revaluation" (First publ. Sept. 1953), *E.M. Forster: 'A Passage to India'*. Ed. Malcolm Bradbury (London: Macmillan, 1970), 136-37.

5. *Ibid.*, 137.

6. *Ibid.*, 138.

7. *Ibid.*, 142-43.

8

E.M. Forster's *A Passage to India* in Jhumpa Lahiri's Short Story, "Interpreter of Maladies"
Susanna Ghazvinizadeh

It has been said that for first generation migrants the return to India will never be like they have imagined it throughout their lives. However, for their children this is not even an *actual* return, since most of them were not even *born* in the subcontinent. Critic Sunaina Maira argues that:

> What is illuminating in second-generation narratives of visits to India is the...recurrent use of the phrase "going back" or "returning".... I interviewed Indian Americans who were born in the United States or elsewhere and who nevertheless spoke of "going back" to places they had never, technically, left. (Maira 112)

Among the few writers who have described the so-called "return" of second generation migrants to South Asia, we may describe Jhumpa Lahiri as the most prominent. She wrote about this theme in a number of short stories and in *The Namesake*, her only novel to-date. Lahiri's aim is to show the complexity of these journeys, also defined "culture missions". Sunaina Maira points out that: "The 'culture mission'...has a ritual dimension, a search for specific knowledge and traditions, that is associated not just with the catalyzing visit-to-India narrative but also with the larger question of what constitutes second-generation ethnic identity" (Maira 110).

In the short story, "Interpreter of Maladies", the title story of the Pulitzer-winning collection of that name, Jhumpa Lahiri writes about one of those journeys: a young husband and wife, Raj and Mina Das, hailing from New Brunswick, New Jersey, are spending a holiday in India with their three children. This short story focuses on a sightseeing trip

the family takes with their guide, Mr. Kapasi, from whose point of view
the story is written.

Kapasi immediately notices the "hybridity" of the family: "The
family looked Indian but dressed as foreigners did" (Lahiri 44) and learns
from the husband that they are part of the growing "breed" of *Indian
Americans*: "Mina and I were both born in America...Born and raised"
(45). The "cultural mission" of these two *Indian Americans* might be
read as a "passage to India" during the era of what Arjun Appadurai has
called the "ethnoscapes" (132), and when one reads this short story, a
number of similarities with E.M. Forster's novel, *A Passage to India* come
to mind. These similarities may help us understand the complexities of
this rite of passage for the children of South Asian migrants. Mr. and
Mrs. Das are visiting India, a country that turns out to be inscrutable to
the Westernized eyes of two Indian Americans, just as it is inscrutable for
two English ladies like Mrs. Moore and Adela Quested. *A Passage to India*
deals with the difficult relationship between British colonizers and India
and the difficult relationship between Indian Americans and India lies
at the core of the story "Interpreter of Maladies" as well. When coming
face to face with this country, second generation migrants like Mina
and Raj Das are as puzzled and bewildered as if they were two travellers
during British colonialism (and it is highly ironic that the husband's
name should be *Raj*). These days the British Empire has been replaced,
so to speak, by the American Empire and Mr. and Mrs. Das might be
considered *third millennium imperial travellers*, but while Mrs. Moore
and Adela Quested are actual foreigners travelling through India, the
Indian American spouses are of South Asian descent: thus in theory they
should be closer to the culture of their parents' country. Their condition
is to be *in-betweens*, which makes them two "Americans born and bred,
almost", to quote a phrase from Hanif Kureishi's *The Buddha of Suburbia*
(3). Homi Bhabha, analyzing the *mimic men* of the British Empire, argues
that they are *almost* like the English, but not *quite*, since they are not truly
English, but *Anglicized* people (Bhabha 86). Perhaps it is because she feels
Americanized but not properly *American* that Mrs. Das is so intrigued
when Mr. Kapasi tells her that his main job is to work as an interpreter of
maladies for a medical doctor: "He (the doctor) has a number of Gujarati
patients. My father was Gujarati, but many people do not speak Gujarati
in this area, including the doctor. And so the doctor asked me to work in
his office, interpreting what the patients say" (Lahiri 50). For Mrs. Das
Kapasi's job is "so romantic" (50), as she puts it, since she unconsciously
sees him as a trope of the idealized India her parents' generation cannot

stop looking back to. Furthermore, Mrs. Das turns to Kapasi because she feels that he might help her understand India just like he helps the doctor understand his patients' illnesses. She is unconsciously searching for her identity. As Sunaina Maira puts it:

> The desire to "return" stems from layers of second-generation experience, many of them imbued with emotional significance, that give rise to wishes to learn more about family history and background, to feel a sense of "belonging", or to resolve conflicting identity issues. (Maira 113)

Mr. Kapasi is an interpreter of maladies, and the "malady" of Mrs. Das is to be a stranger to her family's culture; she does not understand the innuendoes of a phrase from a popular Hindi love song which a man by a tea stall sings to her: "Mr. Kapasi heard one of the shirtless men sing a phrase from a popular Hindi love song as Mrs. Das walked back to the car, but she did not appear to understand the words of the song, for she did not express irritation, or embarrassment, or react in any other way to the man's declarations" (Lahiri 46). Therefore, she turns to Kapasi "the interpreter", since she unconsciously wants him to "translate" India for her: "he would explain things to her, things about India" (Lahiri 59). Salman Rushdie, talking about migrants' states: "The word 'translation' comes, etymologically, from the Latin for 'bearing across'. Having been borne across the world, we are translated men" (Rushdie 17). Eugeen Roosens states that for the children of migrants the journey to their parents' homeland is like a "second migration", or a "radical remigration": a second migration that may take the form of a "psychosocial return to the ethnic group" (Roosens 108). Since Mrs. Das is experiencing a "second migration", she turns to a *translator/interpreter* like Mr. Kapasi, whose job interests her so much, in order to be "translated back" to India. Therefore, during the trip Mrs. Das and Mr. Kapasi draw close to each other and the interpreter starts daydreaming about his new friendship:

> She would write to him, asking about his days interpreting at the doctor's office, and he would respond eloquently, choosing only the most entertaining anecdotes, ones that would make her laugh out loud as she read them in her house in New Jersey. In time she would reveal the disappointment in her marriage, and he his. In this way their friendship would grow, and flourish. (Lahiri 55)

Thinking about Kapasi's feelings about his new friend reminds us of the friendship between Dr. Aziz and Mrs. Moore in *A Passage to India*: the night they meet in the mosque means a lot to Aziz, and he tells Mrs. Moore how much he cherishes a friendship that started in that particular way: "Friendships last longer that begin like that, I think" (Forster 127): while thinking about the English lady and Fielding, he yearns for a never-ending friendship just as Kapasi does:

> It was only when Mrs. Moore or Fielding was near him that he saw further, and knew that it is more blessed to receive than to give. These two had strange and beautiful effects on him—they were his friends, his forever, and he theirs forever; he loved them so much that giving and receiving became one. (Forster 126)

Philosopher Syed Manzurul Islam distinguishes between two types of travellers, the "sedentary traveller" and the "nomadic traveller": the first one interprets travelling "as a machine of othering" (Islam 7) and the latter "is to do with encounters with otherness that fracture both a boundary and an apparatus of representation: it is a performative enactment of be-coming other" (Islam 8). The sedentary traveller moves folded in his home-made codes. His movement amounts to no more than one between fixed lines: departure and arrival between fixed locations that ends up building the process of "othering", that is to say it absorbs the "other" in the recognizable *same*. The sedentary traveller moves his territory along with his body: the "moved body", as Deleuze and Guattari say, that serves as a "portable territory" (Islam 59). The lines through which the sedentary travellers move are called the "rigid lines" which keep them grounded in the enclosure of their home. Despite so many rituals of departure, they cannot really depart. The two lines are a rough sketch of the lines drawn by Deleuze and Guattari. As far as the supple lines are concerned, Islam argues that:

> The supple line does not possess the border of a territory. Hence, on this line one does not reterritorialize, nor does one mark space with an expressive refrain or signify in accordance with the codes of faciality. It breaks boundaries and creates passage. (Islam 60)

According to Syed Manzurul Islam, Mrs. Moore travels through the "supple lines": he interprets the episode in the mosque when she first meets Aziz as a moment in which the English lady encounters the Indian doctor by crossing the frontiers inhabited by the other. She does not treat him as a typical colonizer treats the colonized. Mrs. Moore by travelling through the "supple lines" breaks all boundaries and creates a passage through which she can go toward Aziz without prejudice: "He tells her: 'then you are an Oriental'. She will have a new name, too: Esmiss Esmoor" (Islam 54). As S.M. Islam puts it:

> She encounters him without the insistent memories of the boundaries: it is a meeting without pre-condition. Hence, Mrs. Moore's passage into the mosque is the genuine passage of a traveller. It is also the only moment of encounter with the other without the paranoia of othering. (Islam 54)

According to Kapasi, Mrs. Das, like Mrs. Moore, is travelling following the "supple lines": because of her willingness to approach him; because of her unconscious desire of being "translated back", she does not travel through the "rigid lines" as most tourists do. Kapasi watches her intently and detects in her an authentic interest in what surrounds her: "Mr. Kapasi was pleased that they liked the temple, pleased especially that it appealed to Mrs. Das. She stopped every three or four paces, staring silently at the carved lovers, and the procession of elephants, and the topless female musicians beating on two-sided drums" (Lahiri 57) and above all he notices that while the others are only interested in the sights, she is also interested in *him*, breaking through the rigid lines that divide tourists from their guides: "Mrs. Das was different. Unlike the other women, who had an interest only in the temple, and kept their noses buried in a guidebook, or their eyes behind the lens of a camera, she had taken an interest in him" (Lahiri 58). By crossing the "supple lines" she has a chance of becoming the "other"; and the "other" is represented here by Mr. Kapasi, the *authentic Indian*. It is generally agreed that when the children of South Asian migrants travel to the Indian subcontinent, they are looking for an *authenticity* of sorts. As Sunaina Maira puts it: "Second generation Indian Americans often use visits to India to engage in a specific cultural (and political) project of 'authenticating' their ethnic identity" (Maira 109).

Actually Mrs. Das, just like Adela Quested from *A Passage to India*, is only *on the verge* of crossing the supple lines, but she will not eventually cross them: S.M. Islam writes that in Forster's novel Miss Quested's desire to see "the real India" opens her up to the other for a little while. He also writes that the climax of the novel is in the Marabar Caves episode: between Adela and the cave there no longer rises up the barrier that eternally cuts her off from the "Orient". The only thing Adela has to do is say "yes," and, as S.M. Islam says, she will be "carried through the 'smooth surface' of the passage to the other side" (Islam 52). By saying "yes" she has a chance of becoming a nomadic traveller, but she retraces the barriers she was about to break by asking Aziz a question full of stereotypes, or, as S.M. Islam puts it, a "silly question" (52): "Have you one wife or more than one?" (Forster 136). This trivial question takes Adela back to the route of the rigid lines, back to the spaces of the representation of the other. The same occurs to Mrs. Das when she wastes her chance of crossing the barriers that stand between her and Kapasi's India, in fact she comes up with the revelation that one of her children is not actually her husband's and moreover she expects a *remedy* from Mr. Kapasi:

> I told you because of your talents.... For eight years I haven't been able to express this to anybody, not to friends, certainly not to Raj. He doesn't even suspect it. He thinks I'm still in love with him. Well, don't you have anything to say? ...Mr. Kapasi, don't you have anything to say? I thought that was your job. "My job is to give tours, Mrs. Das." "Not that. Your other job. As an interpreter. ...I was hoping you could help me feel better, say the right thing. Suggest some kind of remedy." (Lahiri 65)

By expecting a remedy from Mr. Kapasi, Mrs. Das slips back to the condition of a sedentary traveller, since all she seems to see in him is the stereotype of the Indian as a *guru* who is capable of solving people's existential problems. Mrs. Das is not able to get rid of her "portable territory" full of orientalistic representations of Indians. Kapasi's reaction is similar to Aziz's reaction when faced with Adela's "silly question": "The question shocked the young man very much.... To ask an educated Indian Moslem how many wives he had-appalling, hideous! ...Damn the English even at their best" (Forster 136). In fact Kapasi feels disparaged by Mrs. Das's demand and realizes that his real patients are superior to her: "Kapasi felt insulted that Mrs. Das should ask him to interpret her common, trivial little secret. She did not resemble the patients in the doctor's office, those who came glassy-eyed and desperate, unable to sleep or breathe or urinate with ease, unable, above all, to give words to their pains" (Lahiri 66).

The climax of "Interpreter of Maladies" is when Kapasi takes the whole family to visit the hills in Udayagiri and Khandagiri: here Mrs. Das loses all hopes of opening up to India. It all happens because of the family's lack of familiarity with the monkeys hanging out in the area:

"Those monkeys give me the creeps" (Lahiri 61), says Mrs. Das, using the same expression as an English character in Forster's novel does while talking about Indians: "He can go where he likes as long as he doesn't come near me. They give me the creeps" (Forster 20) and this makes Mrs. Das more similar to the British colonisers, who Forster describes in terms of "well-developed bodies, fairly developed minds, and undeveloped hearts" (19), than to Indians.

In *Culture and Imperialism* Edward Said highlights how far India is unidentifiable to the English: "Forster's India is a locale frequently described as unapprehensible and too large" (Said 243). He quotes the episode where Adela and her fiancé Ronny watch a bird disappear into a tree, yet they cannot identify it, since, as Forster writes, "nothing in India is identifiable, the mere asking of a question causes it to disappear or to merge in something else" (Forster 86). The Italian critic Silvia Albertazzi, talking about Forster's novel, argues that what makes us understand which characters are really able to succeed in their "rite of passage" is their ability or inability—to interpret the signs of nature (Albertazzi 29). The monkeys in Lahiri's short story are a trope of India's signs of nature, which a second-generation migrant like Mrs. Das has a hard time "figuring out" during what could be considered her rite of passage. At the end of the story she voices her desire to leave: "God, let's get out of here...this place gives me the creeps" (Lahiri 68); and in so doing she breaks the "spell" that was about to turn her into a nomadic traveller. Moreover, by rejecting the monkeys, she is also rejecting their *holiness*, since that particular kind of monkey is called *hanuman*, the name of a crucial character from Hindu mythology: "We call them the hanuman," Mr. Kapasi said. "They are quite common in the area" (Lahiri 47). Albertazzi argues that the sacred element in India seems to manifest itself through animal epiphanies. She also argues that these animals are usually undesirable creatures that only those with a naturally religious soul can recognize as holy (Albertazzi 29). The "animal epiphany" that shocks Mrs. Das so much is symbolized by a bunch of monkeys that surround her son Bobby: "He was surrounded by a group of monkeys, over a dozen of them" (Lahiri 67), and this incident is seen by Mrs. Das simply as an "animal attack", without any special effort on her part to try to understand what these creatures might mean to Indian culture. This attitude denotes a lack of what Albertazzi calls a "religious soul" (29), which in this case means a lack of what Islam calls the "ethics of travel" (3); it means not being able to decipher the space of the elsewhere and its otherness.

In the novel *Red Earth and Pouring Rain* by Vikram Chandra (1995) there is another character who escapes from India because of such "undesirable creatures" as monkeys: Abhay, an Indian university student, has an American girlfriend, Amanda, who, having agreed to visit India with him, decides to go back to the US after running into a monkey: "Amanda was standing in the doorway, backing away from a large red monkey, which was sitting on the table, its tail curled over the teapot, eating a piece of toast" (Chandra 608). In spite of Abhay's efforts to convince her that the monkey is harmless, Amanda keeps on feeling bewildered: " 'Really, they won't do anything. Look.' I touched her shoulder, and walked through the monkeys, they barely moved to give me way on the path, and then I walked back again through them. 'See?' Amanda shook her head" (Chandra 609).

While Abhay is able to "recognize" the monkeys—"While I ate I looked up and saw a white monkey on the roof, I knew him well, he had been stealing things from my parents for years"—(Chandra 613) and to understand their holiness—in fact Hanuman from the *Ramayana* is one of the characters of Chandra's novel—Amanda looks at the monkeys and shakes her head while facing a nature she cannot "figure out". The "real India" that Adela Quested had wanted so much to see is completely different from the stereotyped India Amanda has imagined all along:

> 'Do you know how I imagine it?' she said, eyes still closed. 'Big sky. Green, everything green. Blue water and women in gold saris walking slowly. Everything slow. Birds in trees, parrots. An elephant in the distance, waving its trunk. Unbelievable sunsets.' 'Don't imagine too much,' I said. (Chandra 604)

Amanda, like Mrs. Das or Adela Quested, is not able to travel as nomadic travellers do: as soon as she arrives in Bombay, Abhay tries to explain to her that the Indian metropolis is more than what she sees in front of her eyes: " 'This is Bombay. It's not all like this.' I meant the long line of slums, the cardboard shacks that stretched away from the road" (Chandra 605). Amanda shows her disappointment when she notices that there are no *straight lines* in the city: "Amanda turned to me and she shook her head a little before she spoke. "No. You know, there are no straight lines anywhere" (Chandra 605). The straight lines Amanda yearns for stand for the *rigid lines* that trace a Manichean boundary, dividing the East from the West. On the contrary, it is as though the streets of Bombay were built to suit nomadic travellers; moving through supple lines, opening up to the city's numerous worlds.

It is quite obvious—even though it should not be taken for granted—that Amanda should feel bewildered by India: after all, she is not of South Asian descent. However, for an *in-between* like Mrs. Das who is wavering between being "nomadic" like Mrs. Moore and becoming "sedentary" like Adela Quested, the binary division of the two lines of travelling is only *apparent*. Here, indeed, S.M. Islam argues that rigid and supple lines, striated and smooth spaces, sedentary and nomadic travellers, are not mutually exclusive in actuality (Islam 58).

In the words of Deleuze and Guattari: "Smooth space and striated space—nomad space and sedentary space.... And no sooner have we done that that we must remind ourselves that the two spaces in fact exist only in mixture: smooth space is constantly being translated, traversed into a striated space; striated space is constantly being reversed, overturned to a smooth space" (40). Indeed, this mixture is a peculiarity of the *in-between*.

WORKS CITED

Albertazzi Silvia. *Il tempio e il villaggio: La narrativa indo-inglese contemporanea e la tradizione britannica*. Bologna: Patron, 1978.

Appadurai, Arjuna. *Modernity at Large. Cultural Dimensions of Globalizations*. Minneapolis: U of Minnesota P, 1996.

Bhabha, Homi. *The Location of Culture*. London: Routledge, 1984.

Chandra, Vikram. *Red Earth and Pouring Rain*. London: Faber & Faber, 1995.

Deleuze Gilles, and Félix Guattari. 1980. *A Thousand Plateaux*. London: Athlone Press, 1996.

Forster, E.M. *A Passage to India*. 1924; London: Penguin, 1979.

Islam, Syed M. *The Ethics of Travel From Marco Polo to Kafka*. Manchester: Manchester University Press, 1996.

Kureishi, Hanif. *The Buddha of Suburbia*. London: Faber & Faber, 1990.

Lahiri, Jhumpa. "Interpreter of Maladies." *Interpreter of Maladies*. London: Flamingo, 2000, 43-69.

Maira, Sunaina. *Desis in the House: Indian American Youth Culture in New York City*. Philadelphia: Temple University Press, 2002.

Roosens, Eugeen. *Creating Ethnicity: The Process of Ethnogenesis*. Newbury Park: Sage, 1989.

Rushdie, Salman. "Imaginary Homelands." *Imaginary Homelands*. 1991; London: Penguin, 1992, 9-21.

Said, Edward. *Culture and Imperialism*. London: Vintage, 1993.

9

E.M. Forster's *A Passage to India*: A Study in Ecological Concerns
Ram Narayan Panda

I. ECOLOGICAL PERSPECTIVES

The abundance of ecological content in E.M. Forster's epoch-making novel, *A Passage to India*, eminently warrants that it be studied in terms of suitable methods of eco-critical reading. This paper seeks, in the first place, to explain three important ecological concerns which, respectively, thrust on man, non-human species/entities, and the wholeness of the biosphere. The three positions are explained by anthropocentrism, non-anthropocentrism, and systemicism respectively. Following this, we shall examine the significance of the ecological factors and see how Forster's novel meaningfully addresses each one of these concerns. In the process, an understanding of how 'nature' and 'culture' remain interpenetrated in the novel shall be established while validating the dichotomy of anthropocentrism and non-anthropocentrism in the novel. We shall also seek to understand how colonialism tends to subtly undermine anthropocentrism. And, by way of summing up the findings, we shall see that Forster's novel caters to the notion of "Deep Ecology" which accommodates the three positions stated above.

Two different meanings of the term "ecology" are usually offered: (i) "that division of [399/400] biology which treats of the relations between organisms and their environment; bionomics" and (ii) "the study of human populations and of their reciprocal relations in terms of physical environment, spatial distribution, and cultural characteristics" (*Webster's Comprehensive Dictionary* 399-400). And, it is in relation to the second meaning that "ecology becomes so relevant to study of literatures in particular, and humanities in general. Endorsing this non-scientistic approach, Jonathan Hughes notes:

> The application of the term 'ecology' to humans takes
> it beyond the exclusive realm of biology since...the
> relation between humans and their environment is
> importantly mediated by social and technological
> factors whose study is beyond the scope of that science,
> and it is true also that [8/9] the terms 'ecological' and
> 'environmental' carry different associations, the former
> tending to place more emphasis than the latter on the
> holistic or systemic aspect of organism-environment
> relation. (Hughes 8-9)

Forster's novel, in fact, eminently deserves to be studied as an ur-text
of ecological engagement in conjunction with the other abiding issues
such as colonialism and symbolism among other things. Anyone
venturing into the field of eco-critical study is bound to get lost in the
maze of methodologies developed by several scholars practising the
eco-critical approach. The debate concerning the opposition between
'anthropocentrism' and 'non-anthropocentrism' has largely dominated
the environmental ethics, which is a branch of applied philosophy:

> on the one hand, 'anthropocentrism' which holds
> that only humans are worthy of moral consideration
> for their own sake and that we should preserve
> the environment solely for the sake of the humans
> who inhabit it, and, on the other hand, approaches
> described variously as 'biocentric', 'ecocentric', even
> 'cosmocentric' which ascribe moral considerability to
> some or all of non-human nature. (Hughes 16)

Different positions have been developed around this distinction in
relation to flourishing and moral considerability of sentient and non-
sentient entities. Hughes observes how Reiner Grundmann gives primacy
to the human interest:

> Grundmann's arguments for an anthropocentric
> approach is based on the supposition that the non-
> anthropocentrist must distinguish between states of
> nature which are 'normal' and thus to be preserved,
> and states which are 'pathological' and thus to be
> avoided. Against this, Grundmann objects that it is
> difficult to know what is 'normal' for nature and, more
> strongly that this cannot be defined without reference
> to human interests. (Hughes 20)

The second position has been developed by the "adherents of 'bio-centric' or life-centred ethic such as Robin Attfield and Paul W. Taylor" who "attribute goods of their own to individual living organisms" (21). Hughes, however, observes that moral considerability cannot be extended to a wide range of non-sentient entities having "goods of their own". The third position, developed by ecocentrists such as Baird Callicott and Lawrence Johnson, promotes the idea of the significance of the organisms only in relation to the "collective or 'systemic' entities such as species, eco-systems, and even the biosphere as a whole" (21). The eco-system is viewed "as the primary repository of value, and its component parts (human individuals and others) as valuable only in so far as they contribute to the flourishing of the whole" (22).

Dana Phillips asserts the interrelatedness of nature and culture in general while spelling out the chief questions that ecocriticism should seek to address:

> Nature is thoroughly implicated in culture, and culture is thoroughly implicated in nature. By virtue of my own disciplinary training, the questions all this raises for me are these: what is the truth of ecology in so far as that truth is addressed by literature? How well does literature address that truth? These questions have begun to be asked in Departments of English by ecocriticism. (Phillips 577-78)

On the whole, this paper seeks to study how *A Passage to India* addresses the truth of ecology which is in line with the two questions asked by Phillips in the above quotation. Let us now examine how the ecological factors available in the novel are of tremendous significance.

II. ECOLOGICAL FACTORS IN *PASSAGE*

An unflinching ecological zeal permeates the entire novel with several ecological components having been abundantly used developing a network of intricate relationships. River Ganges stands as a complex symbol of ecological concern, combining "nature" and "culture", and anthropocentrism and non-anthropocentrism alike. In Chapter 1 itself, Forster develops a sense of mutual ecological tolerance between the river and Chandrapore. The river assumes anthropocentric significance in the sense that it continues to put up with the "rubbish" the city "deposits so freely" (Forster, *Passage* 9). But, whenever there is a flood, Chandrapore finds itself at the receiving end: "when Ganges comes down it might be expected to wash the excrescence back into the soil. Houses do fall, people are drowned and left rotting, but the general outline of the town persists, swelling here, shrinking there, like some low but indestructible form of life" (9). But, both nature and culture remain intermingled in the individual identities of both Chandrapore and Ganges. Forster's description of Chandrapore is interwoven with images of nature and culture/society:

> It is a city of Gardens. It is no city, but a forest sparsely scattered with huts. It is a tropical pleasance washed by a noble river. The toddy palms and neem trees and mangoes (9/10) ...rise from the gardens where ancient tanks nourish them, they burst out of stifling purlieus and unconsidered temples seeking light and air, and endowed with more strength than man or his works, they soar above the lower deposit to greet one another with branches and beckoning leaves, and to build a city for the birds. (9-10)

Forster's dichotomous ecological orientation holds together the images of nature testifying to an unbridled strength of nature and the images of culture in "temple" and "city of gardens". Thus, there is to some extent the anthropocentrism of Grundmann whereby nature in the form of the trees have been used to build a "city of gardens" for the benefit of man. Just the way Ganges is used to wash away the filth of Chandrapore or even the "dead bodies floated down...Benares" (32). In keeping with this, Forster seems to develop a strong non-anthropocentrism in terms of the autonomy he grants to nature in the form of the trees, caves, weather, etc. which live in terms of themselves in spite of all human attempts to appropriate them. Even Forster's non-anthropocentrism accommodates the well-being of the crocodiles who do not let "much of a dead body" slip through their jaws to "get down to Chandrapore" (32).

The river has been sufficiently mystified in terms of expressions like "What a terrible river! what a wonderful river!" (32). But, at the same time, Ganges has been demythicized systematically with its religious significance having been placed out of the context: "Ganges happens not to be holy here" (9). Likewise, Marabar Caves have been absolutely cut off from any religious association. Forster elaborately emphasizes human failure to appropriate the caves culturally, with human civilization having failed to leave any "legend of struggle or victory in the Marabar" (124). These are only some instances of manifestation of Forster's non-anthropocentric zeal. Forster's novel is a brilliant study in ecology with man as well as other sentient and non-sentient entities having been granted a peaceful co-existence in dramatization of several instances. Mrs. Moore tenderly approaches a nice little wasp in Ronnie's bungalow, addressing it finally as "pretty dear" (35): "Going to hang up her cloak, she found that the tip of the peg was occupied by a small wasp.... Bats, rats, birds, insects will as soon nest inside a house as out" (35). The horse at the polo maidan, the hyena that causes the car accident, and the elephant that carries the Marabar enthusiasts are only examples of sentient non-human entities, representing nature, finding their way into the cultural domain of man. Likewise, culture in the form of Aziz's cigarette and Mrs. Moore's drink become a part of Marabar symbolizing nature.

Now, we shall examine how colonialism undermines anthropocentrism, in spite of the fact that colonialism as such, as well as in *Passage* is avowedly oriented to civilizing the natives. A branch of non-anthropocentrism, as stated earlier, distinguishes "between states of nature which are 'normal' and thus to be preserved, and states which are pathological and thus to be avoided" (Hughes 20). But, this parameter seems to have been adopted by the haughty Anglo-Indians towards the natives, i.e. human beings instead of nature. Particularly Mrs. Callendar who rather scornfully speaks about the treatment the native patients deserved in the hospitals: "the kindest thing one can do to a native is to let him die" (28). Thus, the application of a cross-methodological/non-anthropocentric approach undermines the anthropocentric thrust to some extent.

III. "DEEP ECOLOGY"

The notion of "Deep Ecology" championed by Arne Naess and George Sessions has as its first principle that "The well-being and flourishing of human and non-human Life of Earth have value in themselves (synonym: intrinsic value, inherent value). These values are independent of the usefulness of the non-human world for human purposes" (Hughes 28). The second important aspect of "Deep Ecology" is the denial of "any basic distinction between self and its environment" involving a blurring of "the distinction between anthropocentric and non-anthropocentric ethics" (Hughes 29). Thus, the first principle of "Deep Ecology" works out a compromise between the 'man-centred' and 'species-centred' positions highlighted earlier on. The second principle of "Deep Ecology" reiterates the systemicist/ 'eco-system-centred' position discussed along with the other two positions. However, since "the denial of a distinction between self and environment is implausible.... Deep Ecologists have gone on to interpret [29/30] the holistic aspect of Deep Ecology in other ways, focusing on the conditions of self-realization rather than those of personal identity" (29-30). In this sense, a strong Deep Ecological awareness runs through the entire novel. If Chandrapore can be seen as representing humanity at large, the relationship between the sky and Chandrapore can be strongly understood along such a line:

> The sky settles everything—not only climates and seasons but when the earth shall be beautiful. By herself she can do little—only feeble outbursts of flowers. But when the sky chooses, glory can rain into the Chandrapore Bazars or a benediction pass from horizon to horizon. The sky can do this because it is so strong and so enormous. (10)

Likewise, at the end of the novel, Aziz's disapproval of the idea of friendship with Fielding until "every blasted Englishman" is driven "into the sea" (317) is only an expression of a macrocosmic reality:

> But the horses didn't want it—they swerved apart; the earth didn't want it, sending up rocks through which riders must pass single file; the temples, the tank, the jail, the palace, the birds, the carrion, the Guest House that came into view as they issued from the gap and saw Mau beneath: they didn't want it, they said in their hundred voices, 'No, not yet,' and the sky said, 'No, not there.' (317)

In a famous essay entitled "Culture and Environment: From Austen to Hardy," Jonathan Bate discusses Austen as an "inheritor of a long tradition of European thought which associated a temperate climate with a liberal society and excessive heat with oriental despotism" (Bate 545). In *Passage*, there is a systematic reenactment of this idea, with the 'Mosque' section, set in temperate weather, permitting repeated attempts at friendship on the part of the relatively liberal Anglo-Indians, whereas with the onset of the Indian summer, which provides the temporal background to the 'Caves' section, the Anglo-Indian authorities assert their haughtiness as McBryde reiterates his theory: "All unfortunate natives are criminals at heart, for the simple reason that they live south of latitude 30°. They are not to blame...we should be like them if we settled here" (164).

While developing his notion of 'broad anthropocentrism', Hughes discusses Grundmann's linking of anthropocentrism and human domination of nature, "while many, even of those who defend an anthropocentric ethic, would want to detach it from the idea of domination, Grundmann suggests that the two go together, as part of the Enlightenment tradition which he sees Marx as representing" (Hughes 30-31). If a society's domination of nature engenders ecological problems for itself, it "can hardly be said to dominate at all" (31), Grundmann argues. In fact, this perception can be applied to Hinduism's positive appropriation of the pepul tree, a form of cultural domination. But, the moment there is any misappropriation at the hands of the subversive forces, there is a threat to humanity at large:

> Mohurram was approaching, and as usual the Chandrapore Mohammedans were building paper towers of a size too large to pass under the branches of a certain pepul tree. One knew what happened next; the tower stuck, a Mohammedan climbed up the pepul and cut the branch off, the Hindus protested, there was a religious riot.... The collector had favoured the Hindus, until he suspected that they had artificially bent the tree nearer the ground. (93)

Likewise, the "Brahminy bull" (58), referred to in Chapter 6, serves a similar purpose. Deifying such sentient or insentient entities, and nurturing them eventually promotes their usefulness, strengthening the roots of anthropocentrism.

Even otherwise, the theme of impossibility of domination of nature has been re-enacted in the entire novel with the Englishmen failing to come to terms with the natural anarchy of the orient as well as its "mystery" or "muddle". The caves symbolize an essence which not only remains impervious to both Mrs. Moore and Adela Quested but overwhelms their cultural upbringing. Such a perception crystallizes, in the context of the novel, a non-anthropocentrism nevertheless. The idea of domination of nature has been subverted in the following lines befitting the allegation about anthropocentrism's suppression of the essentialism enshrined in the structure of non-anthropocentrism: "India is the country, fields, fields, then hills, jungle, hills, and more fields.... How can the mind take hold of such a country? Generations of invaders have tried, but they remain in exile" (135).

However, it may be worthwhile to mention here that we have not highlighted the relevance of another eco-critical approach which relates the poststructuralist notion of instability of meaning to the process of change in nature. This approach, developed by critics like Donald Worster and Joel B. Hagan, may be useful in understanding the possible poststructuralist potential of the novel. As we have seen, the ecology of *Passage* is trichotomous accommodating the three different theoretical positions discussed above which warrant relocating them in the context of Deep Ecology.

WORKS CITED

Bate, Jonathan. "Culture and Environment: From Austen to Hardy", *New Literary History* 30 (1999): 541-60.

Forster, E.M. *A Passage to India*. 1924; Harmondsworth: Penguin Books, 1977.

Hughes, Jonathan. "Ecological Problems: Definition and Evaluation", *Ecology and Historical Materialism*. Cambridge: Cambridge Univeristy Press, 2000. 7-35.

Phillips, Dana. "Ecocriticism, Literary Theory, and Truth of Ecology", *New Literary History* 30 (1999): 577-602.

Webster's Comprehensive Dictionary. International Edition: Vols. I & II. Chicago: J.G. Ferguson Publishing Company, 1984.

10

Forster's Views on Art and the Novel
Vinita Jha

It is in several of his essays, such as 'Anonymity: An Enquiry', 'The Duty of Society to the Artist', 'Art for Art's Sake', 'Does Culture Matter?', '*The Raison d'être* of Criticism in the Arts' and 'Not Listening to Music', that Forster expresses his views on art in general, and it is in his *Aspects of the Novel* that he speaks about the novel in particular. Forster has never claimed to be a literary theorist, nor has he ever tried to evolve his own aesthetics; nevertheless, his views on art are well-defined and consistent.

In his essay entitled 'Art for Art's Sake' Forster says: 'I believe in art for art's sake. It is an unfashionable belief, and some of my statements must be of the nature of an apology.'[1] He goes on to say that 'art for art's sake' is a phrase 'which has been much misused and much abused, but which has...great importance for us—has, indeed, eternal importance.'[2] And it is for this reason that he explains what he means and wants us to understand by this oft-quoted phrase:

> I want...to dismiss...the silly idea that only art matters, an idea which has somehow got mixed up with the idea of art for art's sake, and has helped to discredit it. Many things, besides art, matter. It is merely one of the things that matter, and high though the claims are that I make for it, I want to keep them in proportion.... Art for art's sake does not mean that only art matters.[3]

Forster observes that 'a work of art—whatever else it may be—is a self-contained entity',[4] that it has 'internal order'[5] and 'internal stability',[6] and that this order or stability is 'something evolved from within, not something imposed from without'.[7] He emphasizes this point when he says further that a work of art is 'the one orderly product which our muddling race has produced'.[8] And he goes on to say that a work of art is 'a unique product...not because it is clever or noble or beautiful or enlightened or original or sincere or idealistic or useful or educational— it may embody any of these qualities—but because it is the one material object in the universe which may possess internal harmony'.[9]

It is important to keep in mind that Forster does not speak merely of internal order, stability or harmony in relation to art, he is also conscious, in this regard, of the problem of form. According to him, the artist 'legislates through creating'[10] and that he 'creates through his sensitiveness and his power to impose form'.[11] He says:

> Without form the sensitiveness vanishes. And form is as important today, when the human race is trying to ride the whirlwind, as it ever was in those less agitating days of the past.... Form is not tradition. It alters from generation to generation. Artists always seek a new technique, and will continue to do so as long as their work excites them. But form of some kind is imperative. It is the surface crust of the internal harmony, it is the outward evidence of order.[12]

Forster looks upon internal order or harmony as the soul of a work of art, upon form as its body. He believes in art for art's sake not just in a technical sense but also in a spiritual sense, in the sense that art is an effective instrument of spiritual transformation, that it is an oasis of relief and stability in the desert of panic, emptiness and muddle, and that it is a great testimony of man's creativeness.

It is in his own extraordinary way—we may call it romantic as well— that Forster discusses the nature of the creative process. In 'The Raison d'être of Criticism in the Arts' he observes:

> In it [the creative state] a man is taken out of himself. He lets down as it were a bucket into his subconscious, and draws up something which is normally beyond his reach. He mixes this thing with his normal experiences, and out of the mixture he makes a work of art. It may be a good work of art or a bad one—we are not here examining the question of quality—but whether it is good or bad it will have been compounded in this unusual way, and he will wonder afterwards how he did it. Such seems to be the creative process. It may employ much technical ingenuity and worldly knowledge, it may profit by critical standards, but mixed up with it is

this stuff from the bucket, this subconscious stuff, not procurable on demand.[13]

According to Forster, the creative state of mind is 'akin to a dream'[14]: there is 'conception in sleep, there is the connection between the subconscious and the conscious, which has to be effected before the work of art can be born'.[15] Forster gives due consideration to the importance of technique, of form in the creation of a work of art, but he believes that the moving force behind it is imagination, inspiration, or, may be, intuition. In 'Anonymity: An Enquiry' he observes that creation 'comes from the depths'[16] and that imagination is 'as the immortal God which should assume flesh for the redemption of mortal passion'.[17] He explains this point when he moves from a consideration of art in general to that of literature in particular.

Forster says that books are composed of words and that 'words have two functions to perform: they give information or they create an atmosphere'.[18] And though he accepts that words can and do perform both the functions at one and the same time, he spells out the difference between 'information' and 'creation'. In this connection he says:

> Just as words have two functions—information and creation—so each mind has two personalities, one on the surface, one deeper down. The upper personality has a name.... It is conscious and alert..., and it differs vividly and amusingly from other personalities. The lower personality is a very queer affair. In many ways it is a perfect fool, but without it there is no literature, because unless a man dips a bucket down into it occasionally he cannot produce first-class work.[19]

The creative state of mind, then, is a state of wakeful dream, of inspiration, of excitement. And though some kind of form is imperative for the creation of literature or works of art, the urge to create, the excitement behind creation, is, by its very nature, overwhelming and inescapable. This kind of urge or excitement has nothing to do with what Forster calls 'information'. He is so emphatic about this element of inspiration or excitement behind the creation of literature or works of art that, according to him, even sensitive readers of literature or honest connoisseurs of works of art are transformed into 'minor artists',[20] for 'works of art do have a peculiar pushful quality; the excitement that attended their creation hangs about them, and makes minor artists out of these who have felt their power',[21] He further states that what is 'so wonderful about great literature is that it transforms the man who reads it towards the condition of the man who wrote, and brings to birth in us also the creative impulse'.[22]

Forster speaks of 'information' and 'creation', of the conscious and the subconscious, of technique and imagination, of form and spirit, of the tangible and the indefinable, and thus takes us to the 'double existence'[23] of art or literature. In this regard he says:

> The world created by words exists neither in space nor time though it has semblances of both, it is eternal and indestructible.... We can best define it by negations. It is not this world, its laws are not the laws of science, its conclusions are not those of common sense. And it causes us to suspend our ordinary judgments.[24]

The world of art or literature, maintains Forster, is autonomous; it is governed by its own laws; it exists in time and space, and yet it transcends both. He suggests that there is something else in literature or art besides time and space, which we may call 'value'[25] and which may be realized as 'intensity'.[26] And it is here that he introduces us to the world of music.

Music plays a significant role in Forster's novels. According to Forster, 'music is the deepest of the arts and deep beneath the arts'.[27] He was greatly interested, in music, and loved playing on his piano. It is something really significant that to him 'music...seems to be more real than anything, and to survive when the rest of civilization decays'.[28] He observes:

> Music, more than the other arts, postulates a double existence. It exists in time, and also exists outside time, instantaneously. With no philosophic training, I cannot put my belief clearly, but I can conceive myself hearing a piece as it goes by and also when it has finished. In the latter case I should hear it as an entity, as a piece of sound-architecture, not as a sound-sequence, not as something divisible into bars.[29]

Speaking of his own performances on the piano in 'Not Listening to Music' Forster says that they taught him a little about construction, and gave him 'some notion of the relation of keys'. He states:

> They grow worse yearly, but never will I give them up. For one thing, they compel me to attend—no wool-gathering or thinking myself clever here—and they drain off all non-musical matter. For another thing,

> they teach me a little about construction. I see what
> becomes of a phrase, how it is transformed or returned,
> sometimes bottom upward, and get some notion of the
> relation of keys.[30]

Forster's own performances were neither very deep nor very meaningful, for he was merely an amateur artist, but as a listener he received from music a kind of communication that was indeed profound. This kind of movement could be possible because, according to him, 'there's an insistence in music—expressed largely through rhythm; there's a sense that it is trying to put across at us something which is neither an aesthetic pattern nor a Sermon.'[31]

Forster points out how novelists can profit by music if they care for and try to adopt the kind of beauty inherent in it:

> Music, though it does not employ human beings,
> though it is governed by intricate laws, nevertheless
> does offer in its final expression a kind of beauty which
> fiction might achieve in its own way. Expansion. That
> is the idea the novelist must cling to. Not completion.
> Not rounding off but opening out.[32]

As for himself, Forster is able to translate sounds into colours as well as into states of mind. 'I translated sounds into colours.... The Arts were to be enriched by taking in one another's washing.'[33]

In *Howards End* Forster characterizes Beethoven's fifth symphony as 'sublime noise',[34] and describes how it evokes different impressions and responses in different characters:

> Whether you are like Mrs. Munt, and tap surreptitiously
> when the tunes come—or like Helen, who can see
> heroes and shipwrecks in the music's flood: or like
> Margaret, who can only see the music...in any case, the
> passion of your life becomes more vivid.[35]

Helen Schlegel gets so much absorbed in Beethoven's Symphony, and reads so much of meaning into it, chiefly in relation to her own life, that she is practically lost to the rest of the world, and leaves the Concert Hall excitedly, carrying, absent-mindedly Leonard Bast's umbrella to her house:

The music had summed up to her all that had happened or could happen in her career. She read it as a tangible statement, which could never be superseded. The notes meant this and that to her, and they could have no other meaning, and life could have no other meaning. She pushed right out of the building, and walked slowly down the outside staircase....[36]

In *A Room with a View* Forster tells us about the atmosphere of otherworldliness that music creates: 'the kingdom of music is not the kingdom of this world'.[37] When Lucy Honeychurch finds her life all dull and uninspiring, she plays Beethoven on her piano. And, as we find, Beebe hears in Opus III 'the hammer strokes of victory'.[38]

Forster approaches music, first as music or sound-sequence, and then as suggestion, bringing out the meaning of life, or as atmosphere, evoking states of mind. And it is this very postulate of 'double existence' that governs his discussion of the novel.

II

In the Introductory chapter of *Aspects of the Novel* Forster says: 'I have chosen the title "Aspects" because it is unscientific and vague, because it leaves the maximum of freedom, because it means both the different ways we can look at a novel and the different ways a novelist can look at his work'.[39] And the aspects he takes up for consideration are seven in number: the story, people, the plot, fantasy and prophecy, and pattern and rhythm.

(i) Forster says that 'the fundamental aspect of the novel is its story-telling aspect'[40] without which 'it could not exist'.[41] He defines the story as 'a narrative of events arranged in their time-sequence,[42] and calls it 'the lowest and simplest of literary organisms'.[43] And though he looks upon the story as 'the highest factor common to all novels',[44] he wishes that 'it was not so, that it could be something different—melody, or perception of the truth, not this low atavistic form'.[45]

(ii) With 'people', claims Forster, the novelist's voice acquires a new emphasis which he calls 'emphasis upon value'.[46] He offers his own definition of 'characters' in a novel:

> The novelist...makes up a number of word-masses roughly describing himself..., gives them names or sexes, assigns them plausible gestures, and causes them

> to speak by the use of inverted commas, and perhaps
> to behave consistently. These word-masses are his
> characters.[47]

Forster says that the 'people in a novel can be understood completely by
the reader, if the novelist wishes',[48] and that 'their inner as well as their
outer life can be exposed'.[49] He further states that a character is 'real when
the novelist knows everything about it'.[50] According to him, the novelist
'may not choose to tell us all he knows—many of the facts, even of the
kind we call obvious, may be hidden',[51] but he 'will give us the feeling that
though the character has not been explained, it is explicable, and we get
from this a reality of a kind we can never get in daily life'.[52] Forster divides
fictional characters into 'flat' and 'round' ones. 'Flat' characters are types
or caricatures; they are two-dimensional, and in 'their purest form, they
are constructed round a single idea or quality'.[53] 'Round' characters are
three-dimensional; they are 'capable of surprising us in a convincing
way',[54] and they have 'the incalculability of life about them—life within
the pages of a book'.[55]

   (iii) Forster defines the plot as the novel in 'its logical intellectual
aspect'.[56] He explains his point by bringing out the fundamental difference
between the story and the plot:

> We have defined a story as a narrative of events
> arranged in their time-sequence. A plot is also a
> narrative of events, the emphasis falling on causality.
> The king died and then the queen died', is a story.
> The king died, and then the queen died of grief', is a
> plot. The time-sequence is preserved, but the sense of
> causality overshadows it. Or again: The queen died,
> no one knew why, until it was discovered that it was
> through grief at the death of the king.' This is a plot with
> a mystery in it, a form capable of high development.[57]

Mere curiosity can keep a story going, but, in Forster's view, a plot
'demands intelligence and memory also'.[58] Mystery, which is essential to a
plot, cannot be considered properly and appreciated without intelligence,
and we cannot understand a novel unless we remember the people and
the places and the events in it, unless memory helps us. Forster says that
in a 'fine' plot incident springs out of character, and, having occurred,
alters character to connect events and people closely, so that 'the final
sense...will not be of clues or chains, but of something aesthetically
compact, something which might have been shown straightaway, only

if he had shown it straightaway it would never have become beautiful'.[59] Here Forster discusses what is otherwise known as the organic unity of a novel, and yet he wishes that writers should 'mix themselves up in their material and be rolled over and over by it; that they should not try to subdue any longer, that they should hope to be subdued, to be carried away'.[60] He is not finicky about contrivances, though he is not and cannot be indifferent to them; to him all 'that matters...is whether or not the shifting of attitude and the secret life are convincing'.[61]

(iv) 'There is more in the novel', says Forster, 'than time or people or logic or any of their derivatives',[62] and by 'more', among others, he means fantasy and prophecy, pattern and rhythm. According to him, fantasy brings together 'the kingdoms of magic and nonsense',[63] and 'implies the supernatural, but need not express it'.[64] But whenever it expresses the supernatural, it does so with the help of such devices as 'the introduction of a god, ghost, angel, monkey, monster, midget, witch into ordinary life; or the introduction of ordinary men into no man's land, the future, the past, the interior of the earth, the fourth dimension; or divings into or dividing of personality; or finally the device of parody or adaptation'.[65]

(v) Prophecy is 'an accent in the novelist's voice, an accent for which the flutes and saxophones of fantasy may have prepared us'.[66] Forster says:

> Prophecy—in our sense—is a tone of voice. It may imply any of the faiths that have haunted humanity—Christianity, Buddhism, dualism, Satanism, or the mere raising of human love and hatred to such a power that their normal receptacles no longer contain them; but what particular view of the universe is recommended—with that we are not directly concerned. It is the implication that signifies and will filter into the turns of the novelist's phrase....[67]

Prophecy demands two qualities: 'humility and the suspension of the sense of humour'.[68] Without humility we shall not be able to hear the voice of the prophet, and 'the sense of humour—that is out of place: that estimable adjunct of the educated man must be laid aside'.[69] Prophetic novels, like other novels, deal with the ordinary world, but somehow the people and things in them acquire universal significance. Both prophecy and fantasy are 'alike in having gods';[70] there is in both the sense of mythology; however, prophecy is unlike fantasy, because while 'its face is towards unity,...fantasy glances about',[71] while its 'confusion is incidental,...fantasy's is fundamental'.[72] Prophecy, Forster concludes by saying, 'gives us the sensation of a song or of sound'.[73]

(vi) Pattern, says Forster, 'springs mainly out of the plot, and to which the characters and any other element present also contribute'.[74] It is true that the pattern of a novel appeals to our aesthetic sense, that it causes us to see the book as a whole, but in spite of the merits that pattern has, Forster has his own misgivings about it. He objects to a rigid pattern, because even if it succeeds in externalizing the atmosphere, it 'shuts the doors on life and leaves the novelist doing exercises, generally in the drawing-room'.[75]

(vii) Forster borrows the term 'pattern' from painting, and the term 'rhythm' from music. He speaks of two kinds of 'rhythm', easy and difficult, simple and complex. He defines easy or simple 'rhythm' as 'repetition plus variation',[76] and says that it may be found in a novel in the form of an oft-repeated phrase, haunting us as an echo or a memory, and 'by its lovely waxing and waning [filling] us with surprise and freshness and hope'.[77] The second kind of 'rhythm', difficult or complex, is something which 'some people can hear but no one can tap to'.[78] According to Forster, Beethoven's Fifth Symphony as a whole has this kind of rhythm. And though it is difficult to find 'any parallels for that in fiction, yet it may be present'.[79]

Forster, we see, discusses these aspects of the novel in terms of both technique and value. And though in his opinion the technical or formal aspects of the novel do have their own importance, yet he claims that all novelists, while writing their books, enter 'a common state which it is convenient to call inspiration'.[80] As Wilfred Stone observes, in his book Forster maintains a distinction between 'phenomena and noumena',[81] between what may be called reason and feeling, and yet he connects them and pleads for the 'double existence' of art or literature.

Aspects of the Novel is the published form of Forster's eight lectures, known as the Clark Lectures related to literature, which he delivered at Cambridge in 1927, and the reactions to the book have been both favourable and adverse. While F.R. Leavis who sat through all the lectures was 'astonished at the intellectual nullity that characterized them',[82] H.J. Oliver expresses the view that Forster's book 'must be, even if it is not regarded as a profound aesthetic theory, an illuminating document'.[83] In his turn, Lionel Trilling observes that through in this book 'there are many judgements that are wrong, not because they have travelled a wrong road but because they have persevered far enough on the right road',[84] and yet, according to him, it is 'full of the finest perceptions'.[85]

Aspects of the Novel is indeed a useful book; it discusses a large number of novelists and their works, even if only through hints and suggestions, and though it was not intended to be an exercise in practical or analytical criticism, it is one of the specimens of workshop criticism.

III

Forster believes in art for art's sake, but not in the sense that only art matters; according to him, there are several other things that do also matter, and perhaps matter more importantly. Nevertheless, he looks upon a work of art as a unique product, a self-contained entity, having its own internal order or harmony that evolves from within, not something which is injected into it from without. Forster shows his awareness of the problem of form, of its importance; and form, according to him, is the surface crust of internal harmony, the outward evidence of internal order. He looks upon internal harmony or order as the soul of a work of art, upon form as its body. He believes in art for art's sake, not just in a technical sense but also in a spiritual sense, in the sense that art is an effective instrument of spiritual transformation, an oasis of relief and fulfilment in the desert of panic, emptiness and muddle, as a great tribute to man's creativeness. He speaks of the role of the subconscious in the creation of a work of art, and says that unless normal experiences, worldly knowledge and technical ingenuity are mixed up with the subconscious stuff, it is not possible to create a work of art. He gives due consideration to the importance of technique in the creation of a work of art, but believes that the moving force behind it is imagination, inspiration, or intuition. In other words, as Forster puts it, the creative state of mind is a state of wakeful dream.

Forster speaks of the conscious and the subconscious, of technique and inspiration, of farm and spirit, of the tangible and the indefinable, and thus draws our attention to the double existence of art or literature. The world of art or literature, he maintains, is autonomous; it is governed by its own laws; it exists in time and space, and yet it transcends both. He suggests that there is something else in art or literature besides time and space, which we may call value and which may be realized as intensity. And it is here that Forster comes to music. In his view, music may play a significant role in the creation of art or literature, only if the artist or the writer realizes its beauty and its power of communication, and is able to translate sounds into colours as well as into states of mind.

In *Aspects of the Novel*, once again, Forster takes us to the double existence of art or literature. He proposes, as he says, to 'attack the novel—that spongy tract, those fictions in prose of a certain extent which extend so indiscriminately',[86] not 'with any elaborate apparatus',[87] or with any categorical critical principles or systems, but in terms of 'the human heart'.[88] A novel, says Forster, 'is a work of art, with its own laws, which are not those of daily life',[89] and, in his view, the 'final test of a novel will be our affection for it'.[90] However, the seven aspects of the novel he considers are: the story arousing our curiosity; the characters or people appealing to human feelings and a sense of value; the plot, besides other things, demanding intelligence and also memory; fantasy asking us to pay something extra; prophecy demanding humility and the suspension of our sense of humour; pattern appealing to our aesthetic sense; and rhythm filling us with surprise and freshness and hope. And though Forster discusses these seven aspects, the three of them he shows his predilection for are fantasy, prophecy and rhythm. Still, he demonstrates his commitment to the double existence of art or literature in relation to the novel by considering both its technique and its value.

Aspects of the Novel is an uneven book, and there is in it an irregular kind of movement from the tangible to the abstract. Forster is not a hard-boiled critic, and he considers the novel in his own unusual, personal way, perhaps keeping in mind his own works of fiction. In any case, he does not pay adequate attention to the problem of the point of view in a work of fiction.

NOTES

1. E.M. Forster, *Two Cheers for Democracy* (London, 1951), 98.
2. *Ibid.*, 98.
3. *Ibid.*
4. *Ibid.*, 99.
5. *Ibid.*
6. *Ibid.*
7. *Ibid.*
8. *Ibid.*, 101.
9. *Ibid.*
10. *Ibid.*, 103.
11. *Ibid.*
12. *Ibid.*
13. *Ibid.*, 123.
14. *Ibid.*
15. *Ibid.*, 124.

16.   *Ibid.*, 96.

17.   *Ibid.*, 97.

18.   *Ibid.*, 87.

19.   *Ibid.*, 93.

20.   *Ibid.*, 115.

21.   *Ibid.*, 116.

22.   *Ibid.*, 93.

23.   *Ibid.*, 128.

24.   *Ibid.*, 91.

25.   E.M. Forster, *Aspects of the Novel* (Penguin International edition, 1970), 36.

26.   *Ibid.*

27.   E.M. Forster, *Two Cheers for Democracy* (London, 1951), 117.

28.   *Ibid.*, 138.

29.   *Ibid.*, 128.

30.   *Ibid.*, 138.

31.   *Ibid.*

32.   E.M. Forster, *Aspects of the Novel* (Penguin International edition, 1970), 170.

33.   E.M. Forster, *Two Cheers for Democracy* (London, 1951), 137.

34.   E.M. Forster, *Howards End* (Penguin edition, 1957), 31.

35.   *Ibid.*

36.   *Ibid.*, 34.

37.   E.M. Forster, *A Room with a View* (London, 1958), 40.

38.   *Ibid.*, 41.

39.   E.M. Forster, *Aspects of the Novel* (Penguin International edition, 1970), p. 31.

40.   *Ibid.*, 33.

41.   *Ibid.*, 34.

42.   *Ibid.*, 35.

43.   *Ibid.*

44.   *Ibid.*, 34.

45.   *Ibid.*

46.   *Ibid.*, 51.

47.   *Ibid.*, 52.

48. *Ibid.*, 54.

49. *Ibid.*

50. *Ibid.*, 70.

51. *Ibid.*, 71.

52. *Ibid.*

53. *Ibid.*, 75.

54. *Ibid.*, 85.

55. *Ibid.*

56. *Ibid.*, 103.

57. *Ibid.*, 94.

58. *Ibid.*

59. *Ibid.*, 96.

60. *Ibid.*, 108.

61. *Ibid.*, 92.

62. *Ibid.*, 112.

63. *Ibid.*, 121.

64. *Ibid.*, 117.

65. *Ibid.*, 117-18.

66. *Ibid.*, 129.

67. *Ibid.*, 129-30.

68. *Ibid.*, 130.

69. *Ibid.*

70. *Ibid.*, 115.

71. *Ibid.*, 140.

72. *Ibid.*

73. *Ibid.*

74. *Ibid.*, 151.

75. *Ibid.*, 165.

76. *Ibid.*, 169.

77. *Ibid.*, 168.

78. *Ibid.*, 165.

79. *Ibid.*, 166.

80. *Ibid.*, 28.

81. W. Stone, *The Cave and the Mountain: A Study of E.M. Forster* (Stanford, 1969), 108.

82. Quoted in O. Stallybrass (ed.), *Aspects of the Novel* (Penguin edition, 1977), 13.
83. H.J. Oliver, *The Art of E.M. Forster* (Melbourne, 1962), 13.
84. Lionel Trilling, *E.M. Forster* (London, 1962), 143.
85. *Ibid.*
86. O. Stallybrass (ed.), *Aspects of the Novel* (Penguin edition, 1977), 38.
87. *Ibid.*,
88. *Ibid.*
89. *Ibid.*, 69.
90. *Ibid.*, 38.

Contributors

Reena Mitra, Reader, Department of English, Christ Church P.G. College, Kanpur, Uttar Pradesh.

Sunita Sinha, Department of English, Women's College Samastipur, L.N. Mithila University, Darbhanga, Bihar.

Sreemati Mukherjee, Reader, Department of English, Basanti Devi College, Kolkata, West Bengal.

Shikha Misra, Reader, Depatment of English, C.S.J.M. University, Kanpur, Uttar Pradesh.

Alka Saxena, Reader, Department of English, D.A.V. College, Kanpur, Uttar Pradesh.

Neeta Shukla, Reader, Department of English, D.G. College, Kanpur, Uttar Pradesh.

Nivedita Tandon, Reader, Department of English, D.G. College, Kanpur, Uttar Pradesh.

Susanna Ghazvinizadeh, Centro Letterature Omeoglotte, C/o Dipartimento di Lingue, e Letterature Straniere, Via Cartoleria 5, 40100 Bologna, Italy.

Ram Narayan Panda, Reader in English, Berhampore University, Berhampore, Orissa.

Vinita Jha, M.D.D.M. College, B.R.A. Bihar University, Muzzaffarpur, Bihar.